1/02

24.95

Sexually Transmitted Diseases

Margorie Little

Introduction by C. Everett Koop, M.D., Sc.D.
Former Surgeon General, U.S. Public Health Service

Foreword by Sandra Thurman
Director, Office of National AIDS Policy, The White House

CHELSEA HOUSE PUBLISHERS
Philadelphia

The goal of the 21ST CENTURY HEALTH AND WELLNESS is to provide general information in the ever-changing areas of physiology, psychology, and related medical issues. The titles in this series are not intended to take the place of the professional advice of a physician or other health-care professional.

Chelsea House Publishers
EDITOR IN CHIEF: Stephen Reginald
MANAGING EDITOR: James D. Gallagher
PRODUCTION MANAGER: Pam Loos
ART DIRECTOR: Sara Davis
DIRECTOR OF PHOTOGRAPHY: Judy Hasday
SENIOR PRODUCTION EDITOR: Lee Anne Gelletly
ASSISTANT EDITOR: Anne Hill
PRODUCTION SERVICES: Pre-Press Company, Inc.
COVER DESIGNER/ILLUSTRATOR: Emiliano Begnardi

The Chelsea House World Wide Web site address is http://www.chelseahouse.com

3 5 7 9 8 6 4 2

Library of Congress Cataloging-in-Publication Data

Little, Marjorie.
Sexually transmitted diseases/ by Marjorie Little.
p.   cm. — (21st century health and wellness)
Originally published: New York: Chelsea House, 1991.
Includes bibliographical references and index.
Summary: Discusses the symptoms, diagnosis, treatment, and complications of such diseases as syphilis, gonorrhea, herpes, and HIV.
ISBN 0-7910-5528-0
1. Sexually transmitted diseases—Juvenile literature. [1. Sexually transmitted diseases. 2. Diseases.] I. Title. II. Series.
RC200.25 .I588 1999
619.95'1—dc21

99-051966

616.951
LIT
2000

CONTENTS

- AIDS
- Allergies
- The Circulatory System
- The Digestive System
- The Immune System
- Mononucleosis and Other Infectious Diseases
- Organ Transplants
- Pregnancy & Birth
- The Respiratory System
- Sexually Transmitted Diseases
- Sports Medicine

PREVENTION AND EDUCATION: THE KEYS TO GOOD HEALTH

C. Everett Koop, M.D., Sc.D.
FORMER SURGEON GENERAL,
U.S. Public Health Service

The issue of health education has received particular attention in recent years because of the presence of AIDS in the news. But our response to this particular tragedy points up a number of broader issues that doctors, public health officials, educators, and the public face. In particular, it spotlights the importance of sound health education for citizens of all ages.

Over the past 35 years, this country has been able to achieve dramatic declines in the death rates from heart disease, stroke, accidents, and—for people under the age of 45—cancer. Today, Americans generally eat better and take better care of themselves than ever before. Thus, with the help of modern science and technology, they have a better chance of surviving serious—even catastrophic—illnesses. In 1996, the life expectancy of Americans reached an all-time high of 76.1 years. That's the good news.

The flip side of this advance has special significance for young adults. According to a report issued in 1998 by the U.S. Department of Health and Human Services, levels of wealth and education in the United States are directly correlated with our population's health. The more money Americans make and the more years of schooling they have, the better their health will be. Furthermore, income inequality increased in the U.S. between 1970 and 1996. Basically, the rich got richer—people in high income brackets had greater increases in the amount of money made than did those at low income levels. In addition, the report indicated that children under 18 are more likely to live in poverty than the population as a whole.

Family income rises with each higher level of education for both men and women from every ethnic and racial background. Life expectancy, too, is related to family income. People with lower incomes tend to die at younger ages than people from more affluent homes. What all this means is that health is a factor of wealth and education, both of which need to be improved for all Americans if the promise of life, liberty, and the pursuit of happiness is to include an equal chance for good health.

The health of young people is further threatened by violent death and injury, alcohol and drug abuse, unwanted pregnancies, and sexually transmitted diseases. Adolescents are particularly vulnerable because they are beginning to explore their own sexuality and perhaps to experiment with drugs and alcohol. We need to educate young people to avoid serious dangers to their health. The price of neglect is high.

Even for the population as a whole, health is still far from what it could be. Why? Most death and disease are attributed to four broad elements: inadequacies in the health-care system, behavioral factors or unhealthy lifestyles, environmental hazards, and human biological factors. These categories are also influenced by individual resources. For example, low birth weight and infant mortality are more common among the children of less educated mothers. Likewise, women with more education are more likely to obtain prenatal care during pregnancy. Mothers with fewer than 12 years of education are almost 10 times more likely to smoke during pregnancy—and new studies find excessive aggression later in life as well as other physical ailments among the children of smokers. In short, poor people with less education are more likely to smoke cigarettes, which endangers health and shortens the life span. About a third of the children who begin smoking will eventually have their lives cut short because of this practice.

Similarly, poor children are exposed more often to environmental lead, which causes a wide range of physical and mental problems. Sedentary lifestyles are also more common among teens with lower family income than among wealthier adolescents. Being overweight—a condition associated with physical inactivity as well as excessive caloric intake—is also more among poor, non-Hispanic, white adolescents. Children from rich families are more likely to have health insurance. Therefore, they are more apt to receive vaccinations and other forms of early preventative medicine and treatment. The bottom line is that kids from lower income groups receive less adequate health care.

To be sure, some diseases are still beyond the control of even the most advanced medical techniques that our richest citizens can afford. Despite yearnings that are as old as the human race itself, there is no "fountain of youth" to prevent aging and death. Still, solutions are available for many of the problems that undermine sound health. In a word, that solution is prevention. Prevention, which includes health promotion and education, can save lives, improve the quality of life, and, in the long run, save money.

In the United States, organized public health activities and preventative medicine have a long history. Important milestones include the improvement of sanitary procedures and the development of pasteurized milk in the late-19th century, and the introduction in the mid-20th century of effective vaccines against polio, measles, German measles, mumps, and other once-rampant diseases. Internationally, organized public health efforts began on a wide-scale basis with the International Sanitary Conference of 1851, to which 12 nations sent representatives. The World Health Organization, founded in 1948, continues these efforts under the aegis of the United Nations, with particular emphasis on combating communicable diseases and the training of health-care workers.

Despite these accomplishments, much remains to be done in the field of prevention. For too long, we have had a medical system that is science and technology-based, and focuses essentially on illness and mortality. It is now patently obvious that both the social and the economic costs of such a system are becoming insupportable.

Implementing prevention and its corollaries, health education and health promotion, is the job of several groups of people. First, the medical and scientific professions need to continue basic scientific research, and here we are making considerable progress. But increased concern with prevention will also have a decided impact on how primary-care doctors practice medicine. With a shift to health-based rather than morbidity-based medicine, the role of the "new physician" includes a healthy dose of patient education.

Second, practitioners of the social and behavioral sciences—psychologists, economists, and city planners along with lawyers, business leaders, and government officials—must solve the practical and ethical dilemmas confronting us: poverty, crime, civil rights, literacy, education, employment, housing, sanitation, environmental protection, health-care delivery systems, and so forth. All of these issues affect public health.

Third is the public at large. We consider this group to be important in any movement. Fourth, and the linchpin in this effort, is the public health profession: doctors, epidemiologists, teachers—who must harness the professional expertise of the first two groups and the common sense and cooperation of the third: the public. They must define the problems statistically and qualitatively and then help set priorities for finding solutions.

To a very large extent, improving health statistics is the responsiblity of every individual. So let's consider more specifically what the role of the individual should be and why health education is so important. First, and most obviously, individuals can protect themselves from illness and injury and thus minimize the need for professional medical care. They can eat a nutritious diet; get adequate exercise; avoid tobacco, alcohol, and drugs; and take prudent steps to avoid accidents. The proverbial "apple a day keeps the doctor away" is not so far from the truth, after all.

Second, individuals should actively participate in their own medical care. They should schedule regular medical and dental checkups. If an illness or injury develops, they should know when to treat themselves and when to seek professional help. To gain the maximum benefit from any medical treatment, individuals must become partners in treatment. For instance, they should understand the effects and side effects of medications. I counsel young physicians that there is no such thing as too much information when talking with patients. But the corollary is the patient must know enough about the nuts and bolts of the healing process to understand what the doctor is telling him or her. That responsibility is at least partially the patient's.

Education is equally necessary for us to understand the ethical and public policy issues in health care today. Sometimes individuals will encounter these issues in making decisions about their own treatment or that of family members. Other citizens may encounter them as jurors in medical malpractice cases. But we all become involved, indirectly, when we elect our public officials, from school board members to the president. Should surrogate parenting be legal? To what extent is drug testing desirable, legal, or necessary? Should there be public funding for family planning, hospitals, various types of medical research, and medical care for the indigent? How should we allocate scant technological resources, such as kidney dialysis and organ transplants? What is the proper role of government in protecting the rights of patients?

What are the broad goals of public health in the United States today? The Public Health Service has defined these goals in terms of mortality, education, and health improvement. It identified 15 major concerns: controlling high blood pressure, improving family planning, pregnancy care and infant health, increasing the rate of immunization, controlling sexually transmitted diseases, controlling the presence of toxic agents or radiation in the environment, improving occupational safety and health, preventing accidents, promoting water fluoridation and dental health, controlling infectious diseases, decreasing smoking, decreasing alcohol and drug abuse, improving nutrition, promoting physical fitness and exercise, and controlling stress and violent behavior. Great progress has been made in many of these areas. For example, the report *Health, United States, 1998* indicates that in general, the workplace is safer today than it was a decade ago. Between 1980 and 1993, the overall death rate from occupational injuries dropped 45 percent to 4.2 deaths per 100,000 workers.

For healthy adolescents and young adults (ages 15 to 24), the specific goal defined by the Public Health Service was a 20% reduction in deaths, with a special focus on motor vehicle injuries as well as alcohol and drug abuse. For adults (ages 25 to 64), the aim was 25% fewer deaths, with a concentration on heart attacks, strokes, and cancers. In the 1999 National Drug Control Strategy, the White House Office of National Drug Control Policy echoed the Congressional goal of reducing drug use by 50 percent in the coming decade.

Smoking is perhaps the best example of how individual behavior can have a direct impact on health. Today cigarette smoking is recognized as the most important single preventable cause of death in our society. It is responsible for more cancers and more cancer deaths than any other known agent; is a prime risk factor for heart and blood vessel disease, chronic bronchitis, and emphysema; and is a frequent cause of complications in pregnancies and of babies born prematurely, underweight, or with potentially fatal respiratory and cardiovascular problems.

Since the release of the Surgeon General's first report on smoking in 1964, the proportion of adult smokers has declined substantially, from 43% in 1965 to 30.5% in 1985. The rate of cigarette smoking among adults declined from 1974 to 1995, but rates of decline were greater among the more educated. Since 1965, more than 50 million people have quit smoking. Although the rate of adult smoking has decreased, children and teenagers are smoking more. Researchers have also noted a disturbing correlation between underage smoking of cigarettes and later use of cocaine and heroin. Although there is still much work to be done if we are to become a "smoke free society," it is heartening to note that public health and public education efforts—such as warnings on cigarette packages, bans on broadcast advertising, removal of billboards advertising cigarettes, and anti-drug youth campaigns in the media—have already had significant effects.

In 1997, the first leveling off of drug use since 1992 was found in eighth graders, with marijuana use in the past month declining to 10 percent. The percentage of eighth graders who drink alcohol or smoke cigarettes also decreased slightly in 1997. In 1994 and 1995, there were more than 142,000 cocaine-related emergency-room episodes per year, the highest number ever reported since these events were tracked starting in 1978. Illegal drugs present a serious threat to Americans who use these drugs. Addiction is a chronic, relapsing disease that changes the chemistry of the brain in harmful ways. The abuse of inhalants and solvents found in legal products like hair spray, paint thinner, and industrial cleaners—called "huffing" (through the mouth) or "sniffing" (through the nose)—has come to public attention in recent years. *The National Household Survey on Drug Abuse* discovered that among youngsters ages 12 to 17, this dangerous practice doubled between 1991 and 1996 from 10.3 percent to 21 percent. An alarming large number of children died the very first time they tried inhalants, which can also cause brain damage or injure other vital organs.

Another threat to public health comes from firearm injuries. Fortunately, the number of such assaults declined between 1993 and 1996. Nevertheless, excessive violence in our culture—as depicted in the mass media—may have contributed to the random shootings at Columbine High School in Littleton, Colorado, and elsewhere. The government and private citizens are rethinking how to reduce the fascination with violence so that America can become a safer, healthier place to live.

The "smart money" is on improving health care for everyone. Only recently did we realize that the gap between the "haves" and "have-nots" had a significant health component. One more reason to invest in education is that schooling produces better health.

In 1835, Alexis de Tocqueville, a French visitor to America, wrote, "In America, the passion for physical well-being is general." Today, as then, health and fitness are front-page items. But with the greater scientific and technological resources now available to us, we are in a far stronger position to make good health care available to everyone. With the greater technological threats to us as we approach the 21st century, the need to do so is more urgent than ever before. Comprehensive information about basic biology, preventative medicine, medical and surgical treatments, and related ethical and public policy issues can help you arm yourself with adequate knowledge to be healthy throughout life.

FOREWORD

Sandra Thurman, Director, Office of National AIDS Policy, The White House

A hundred years ago, an era was marked by discovery, invention, and the infinite possibilities of progress. Nothing peaked society's curiosity more than the mysterious workings of the human body. They poked and prodded, experimented with new remedies and discarded old ones, increased longevity and reduced death rates. But not even the most enterprising minds of the day could have dreamed of the advancements that would soon become our shared reality. Could they have envisioned that we would vaccinate millions of children against polio? Ward off the annoyance of allergy season with a single pill? Or give life to a heart that had stopped keeping time?

As we stand on the brink of a new millennium, the progress made during the last hundred years is indeed staggering. And we continue to push forward every minute of every day. We now exist in a working global community, blasting through cyber-space at the speed of light, sharing knowledge and up-to-the-minute technology. We are in a unique position to benefit from the world's rich fabric of traditional healing practices while continuing to explore advances in modern medicine. In the halls of our medical schools, tomorrow's healers are learning to appreciate the complexities of our whole person. We are not only keeping people alive, we are keeping them well.

Although we deserve to rejoice in our progress, we must also remember that our health remains a complex web. Our world changes with each step forward and we are continuously faced with new threats to our well-being. The air we breathe has become polluted, the water tainted, and new killers have emerged to challenge us in ways we are just beginning to understand. AIDS, in particular, continues to tighten its grip on America's most fragile communities, and place our next generation in jeopardy.

Facing these new challenges will require us to find inventive ways to stay healthy. We already know the dangers of alcohol, smoking and drug abuse. We also understand the benefits of early detection for illnesses like cancer and heart disease, two areas where scientists have made significant in-roads to treatment. We have become a well-informed society, and with that information comes a renewed emphasis on preventative care and a sense of personal responsibility to care for both ourselves and those who need our help.

Read. Re-read. Study. Explore the amazing working machine that is the human body. Share with your friends and your families what you have learned. It is up to all of us living together as a community to care for our well-being, and to continue working for a healthier quality of life.

1

STDs TODAY

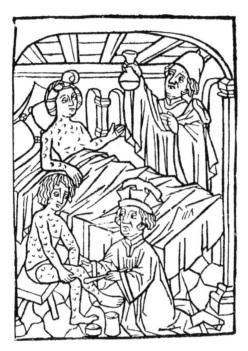

Some sexually transmitted diseases such as syphilis, have existed since at least the beginning of recorded history.

In the United States today, there is an epidemic of sexually transmitted diseases. More than 12 million new cases of these infections, also known as STDs, occur every year. Of all age groups, people from 15 to 24 years old make up the largest segment infected with STDs. Almost two-thirds of all reported cases occur among people less than 25 years old.

At least 20 different STDs have been identified. Whereas some, such as *syphilis,* are at least as old as recorded history, others, such as *AIDS* (acquired immune deficiency syndrome), have only recently been identified. All STDs, however, are highly contagious and are spread primarily through the intimate physical contact of sexual activity. *Herpes* and *genital warts,* two common STDs, are most often spread through direct exposure to infected skin.

Others, such as syphilis, *gonorrhea,* and *chlamydia,* can be transmitted through contact with infected blood, vaginal secretions, or semen (a mixture of sperm and fluids secreted by the body). It is extremely unlikely, if not impossible, to contract an STD from a toilet seat, a towel, or anything else touched by an infected person.

Most STDs can be treated and cured. If not treated, however, serious complications can develop: permanent damage to reproductive organs, blindness, chronic illness, heart disease, a greater risk of cancer, or even death. Two STDs remain incurable. One is herpes, a painful infection

Photo montage showing various aspects of a venereal disease clinic in South Carolina, 1944. Just three years earlier it had been discovered that penicillin could provide a quick and effective cure for syphilis.

suffered by millions of Americans. Although herpes symptoms can be treated, there is still no way to prevent the initial infection or stop recurring outbreaks. The second incurable STD is AIDS—the most life threatening of all. AIDS is the final and most serious stage of infection caused by *human immunodeficiency virus,* also known as HIV. This virus destroys cells of the immune system, making it increasingly difficult for the body to fight off infections or diseases, such as pneumonia and cancer.

WHO IS AT RISK?

STDs affect single people, married people, heterosexuals, bisexuals, homosexuals, and people of all races, religions, and economic backgrounds. Anyone who is sexually active may be at risk. Males can give STDs to female or male sexual partners. Females can infect male sexual partners, female partners, and their own unborn children.

GENERAL SYMPTOMS

Some symptoms that may indicate an STD infection include

- Sores, growths, rashes, or blisters on sex organs, the anus, or the mouth.
- Pain or burning during urination.
- Pain during sexual intercourse.
- Swelling or itching in the genital or anal area.
- Unusual discharge from the vagina or penis.

Anyone who develops at least one of these symptoms should visit a doctor or health clinic for a medical examination and testing. In addition, a person who believes that he or she may have been exposed to an STD should also seek immediate medical attention rather than wait for signs to develop. Often there will not be any noticeable symptoms in the early stage of disease. Signs of a sexually transmitted infection may also appear and then disappear without any treatment. This does not mean, however, that a spontaneous cure has occurred. Unlike colds and measles, STDs usually do not go away without medical attention.

As with most infectious diseases, STDs respond best to early detec-

Researchers around the world are searching for effective AIDS treatments and vaccines.

tion and treatment. Many doctors feel that everyone who is sexually active, particularly those who have more than one partner, should schedule routine, periodic examinations as an extra precaution. Most STDs are extremely contagious even if the infected person is free of symptoms.

PREVENTION

There are only two groups of people who can be fairly sure they will not get an infection through sexual intimacy. The first includes people who are celibate. This group does not have sex. The other group is made up of uninfected individuals who are monogamous. For this to be an effective defense against STDs, the partner must also be uninfected and monogamous.

Among people who are neither celibate nor monogamous, the risk factor depends on how carefully they select their partners and their choice of sexual activities. Having multiple partners or even having just one partner who is sexually active with other people increases the possibility of exposure to STDs. This risk can be minimized by learning about these infections, knowing what to ask potential lovers, and understanding safer-sex techniques.

Having an active sex life that is both satisfying and healthy involves issues of choice and responsibility. Stopping the epidemic of STDs requires that people have access to information about these illnesses. This book was written with both goals in mind.

2

STDs THROUGH THE AGES

Venereal disease has stalked the famous and the infamous. It was syphilis, not bullets, that finally cut down ruthless Chicago mobster Al Capone.

Researchers are still uncertain as to when the first STD appeared. Many argue that these illnesses are as old as sexual intercourse. The first written record, a description of the symptoms of syphilis, dates back to a Chinese medical report from 2000 B.C.

Until the late 18th century, scientists thought that all sexually transmitted infections were the same disease. They called it *venereal disease*, or VD. Although experts were slow to recognize that there was more than one kind of VD, they did pinpoint the method of contagion: The word *venereal is* derived from Venus, the Roman goddess of love.

DISEASE OF THE FAMOUS AND INFAMOUS

In examining old documents, researchers have been able to identify many early sufferers of the "infections of Venus." In some cases, venereal disease is thought to have changed the fate of nations. Henry VIII, the king of England from 1509 to 1547, is often used as a tragic example. An extremely cruel monarch, Henry VIII was believed to be responsible for the murder of several of his wives as well as approximately 3% of the entire population of London.

According to a popular diagnosis reviewed in Theodor Rosebury's book *Microbes and Morals,* published by Viking Press in 1971, the king's actions were prompted by insanity resulting from an advanced case of syphilis. This is not surprising, as court documents throughout his reign indicate that Henry frequently engaged the services of prostitutes and that he suffered from a wide range of complaints characteristic of syphilis. His daughter Mary exhibited many of the telltale physical symptoms common to children of syphilitic parents, such as a grotesquely protruding forehead, baldness, and bad eyesight.

Biographical records indicate that Julius Caesar, Cleopatra, Emperor Charlemagne, Frederick the Great of Prussia, Catherine the Great of Russia, and Napoléon Bonaparte are among the many world leaders who had firsthand experience with the symptoms of venereal disease. Then, as now, no one who was sexually active was invincible—not even dictators. Adolf Hitler apparently suffered from syphilis throughout his life, and Benito Mussolini had both syphilis and gonorrhea. In addition, syphilis claimed the life of Chicago mobster Al Capone. Acccording to Robert Helmer, M.D., in his book *Venus Dilemma* (Nash Publishers, 1974), historians have revealed that Woodrow Wilson, the 28th president of the United States, also suffered from the disease. Apparently, Wilson was exposed to syphilis as a young man and carried the infection for years. It is thought that the crippling, incapacitating paralysis that marked his last two years as president was caused by advanced syphilis.

The list goes on and on. Poets, clergy, painters, writers, statesmen, musicians, and philosophers as well as the poor, the enslaved, the women of the streets, the rich, the working class, the ordinary, the extraordinary, the ignorant, and the educated are all represented.

ORIGINS OF STD

For centuries historians have argued as to who was responsible for introducing venereal disease to European civilization, and the debate still rages. Most agree, however, that VD was already present in Europe during the Middle Ages. Records show that by the 12th century, authorities in England were attempting to control the spread of venereal disease by trying to abolish prostitution and by isolating patients diagnosed with VD. Under local ordinance, this isolation often meant physical removal of infected patients from their communities. For hundreds of years, however, VD did not seem to be particularly widespread, and the strains being transmitted do not appear to have been especially life threatening.

Suddenly, at the end of the 15th century, venereal disease spread wildly across Europe. Many historians believe that the exploits of Charles VIII of France started this devastating epidemic. In 1494, Charles amassed an army of mercenaries and crossed the Alps in an attempt to capture the throne of Naples. Charles and his men invaded Italy, where they were met by defending troops. As was common, a sizable population of camp followers, many of whom were prostitutes,

Venereal disease has exercised a profound effect on history. French emperor Napoléon Bonaparte, U.S. president Woodrow Wilson, and European dictators Adolf Hitler and Benito Mussolini are all thought to have suffered from sexually transmitted illness.

accompanied both armies. Within six months, a particularly severe form of VD had nearly devastated both sides. Charles was forced to give up his siege and dismiss his men. As his troops headed home, they transmitted the disease in Germany, France, Switzerland, Holland, Greece, England, and Portugal. Within a few years, explorers had spread this apparently new strain even farther to the people of India, China, and Japan.

The plague that resulted acquired many names. The Italians and English called it the French Disease; the French called it the Neapolitan, or Italian, Disease; the Germans called it the French Pox; the Dutch and the Portuguese called it the Spanish Disease. Obviously, no one wanted to claim responsibility.

Girolamo Fracastorius, an Italian poet and doctor, was the first to call this disease syphilis. The name appeared in his poem "Syphilis: or, a poetical History of the French Disease," published in 1530. In this work, a young pig herder named Syphilis angers the god Apollo by building

British monarch Henry VIII apparently suffered from venereal disease, and his daughter Mary showed symptoms common to children of syphilitic parents. These include baldness, poor vision, and a protruding forehead.

forbidden altars on sacred ground. To punish the foolish mortal, Apollo inflicts him with a horrible disease that causes his entire body to break out in painful, ulcerating sores. From this point until the late 18th century, all venereal disease was commonly called syphilis.

A MEDICAL MYSTERY

The belief that all STD symptoms could be caused by the same disease was reinforced by the work of the well-respected physician John Hunter. In 1767, Hunter set out to prove that different venereal disease symptoms were not an indication that more than one disease existed but were simply related to where the disease entered the body. Hunter believed that if the disease entered the *urethra*, the opening through which urine passes, the patient developed symptoms of what is today known as gonorrhea. If infection originated on the external skin of the penis, it became a syphilitic ulcer.

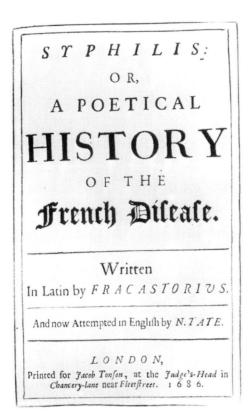

Cover from an early English-language edition of the poem that coined the word syphilis.

To prove his point, Hunter took pus from a patient who had gonorrhea and placed it in his own urethra. In less than a week the physician developed gonorrhea. Within four weeks he also developed the skin rash associated with syphilis. Hunter believed that this proved conclusively that gonorrhea and syphilis were two manifestations of the same disease. His experiment was doubly unfortunate: Hunter's patient had both gonorrhea and syphilis, and the pus carried both infections. The syphilis that the unwitting Hunter contracted to prove his hypothesis caused his death.

Because Hunter had such an impressive reputation, however, his mistaken theory was accepted for more than two decades. In 1793, Benjamin Bell, a Scottish scientist, proved that Hunter was wrong and that syphilis and gonorrhea were two separate diseases. Bell was also slightly more advanced in the design of his study. He used medical students as guinea pigs rather than himself. Phillipe Ricord, a French scientist, confirmed the results of Bell's work. In 1837, Ricord was among the first physicians to recognize that syphilis could progress through three stages.

Experiments by William Wallace, a scientist working in Dublin in the early 19th century, proved that contact with a syphilitic skin rash could also spread the disease. This rash most frequently occurs after the initial symptoms of syphilis disappear. Wallace used poor people who showed up at public clinics as subjects for his experiments. It is very unlikely that these people were given any choice or informed that they were to be infected with syphilis.

Although current medical studies are designed with great care to prevent the exploitation of human subjects, this was not always the case. In the past, some experiments that were conducted, such as those by Bell and Wallace, would today seem scandalous. One of most infamous was the Tuskegee Study, an experiment designed to show the long-term effects of untreated syphilis. The study began in 1932, and 400 black men were recruited as subjects. All were diagnosed as being ill with syphilis and were promised free care. The men were not informed, however, that they were part of an experiment. Nor were they told that some of them would get care that was intentionally useless in the treatment of their disease.

As the study progressed, so did the syphilis of the Tuskegee subjects. The project continued for 40 years, long after penicillin became widely recognized and widely available as a cure for syphilis. In 1972, the study

John Hunter, a respected 18th-century physician, mistakenly believed that syphilis and gonorrhea were the same disease. Attempting to prove his theory, he experimented on himself and contracted a fatal case of syphilis.

received national public attention and was stopped. Unfortunately, only 74 of the original subjects were still alive. It is estimated that between 28 and 100 had died as a direct result of advanced syphilis. No one knows how many lives could have been saved if patients had been given proper treatment when it became available.

A. M. Brandt, a medical investigator, wrote in *The Hastings Center Report* in 1978 that the Tuskegee Study "revealed more about the pathology of racism than it did about the pathology of syphilis."

EARLY TREATMENT ATTEMPTS

Until the development of modern antibiotics, the treatment of sexually transmitted infections was often worse than the diseases themselves. From ancient times until the end of the 18th century, catheters were used to "irrigate" the sexual organs of infected men. These narrow tubes were inserted into the urethra and various liquids were then forced up into the organ.

Even Bell, the physician who first recognized that VD was more than one disease, was a great promoter of urethral irrigations. According to Allan Chase in his book *The Truth about STD,* published by Quill in 1983, Bell often prescribed 3 to 10 infusions a day for patients with gonorrhea who came to him in the late 1790s. Bell recommended using a mixture containing mild acids and strong spirits such as brandy mixed with water.

Although catheters were eventually replaced by hand-held and pressurized syringes, urethral infusions remained popular until well into the 20th century.

Other popular therapies for venereal disease were not only painful but also highly poisonous. This was certainly true of mercury, which was used until the middle of the 20th century. Mercury was administered in almost every way possible and usually for a very long time. "One night with Venus, a lifetime with Mercury" was a popular refrain among patients.

Some practitioners combined mercury with lard or oil and then instructed their patients to rub the salve directly onto their sores. Others prescribed mercury in pill form; still other physicians used fumigation. In this procedure the patient was covered with mercury-soaked rags and then locked in a closed cabinet with just his or her head sticking out. A fire was built below to heat the mercury. As it vaporized, the mercury rose and was inhaled by the patient. Mercury was also injected directly into sexual organs and lesions.

Although there was some documented proof of the benefits of mercury therapy, far more was written about the horrible side effects. Included are reports of severe ulcerations of the mouth, loss of teeth, stomach and digestive disorders, bone loss, and death. The German poet Ulrich von Hutten (1488–1523) was one of the first victims of mercury mistreatment to write about it. In *Syphilis and Other Venereal Diseases,* published by Harvard University Press in 1973, William Brown records the trials von Hutten suffered.

According to the poet, his jaws, tongue, lips, and palate became ulcerated, his gums swelled, and his teeth loosened and fell out. Saliva dripped continuously from his mouth, and his breath became intolerably fetid. To make matters worse, von Hutten apparently suffered a relapse of syphilis.

Early attempts to treat venereal disease proved both painful and dangerous and often provided little or no benefit.

PREVENTION

By the end of the 18th century, it was quite obvious that venereal disease was out of control and spreading rapidly, particularly among soldiers. Authorities attempted to control the disease by eliminating prostitution. When all efforts to outlaw, banish, and jail prostitutes failed, officials tried a new approach. They passed legislation requiring prostitutes to register with authorities and undergo routine health inspections. Although registration was widespread in Europe, in the United States only St. Louis and Cincinnati tried it. This, too, was ineffective: Most prostitutes did not sign up. Many who did became infected with VD as a result of being examined by doctors who did not sterilize instruments between patients. Many doctors had no idea what they were looking for or how to treat VD when they found it.

By the beginning of the 20th century, the Social Hygiene Movement, also called the Purity Crusade, was launched in the United States and Europe. This movement attracted an enormous variety of people determined to eliminate VD. Although they agreed on the goal, there was considerable difference of opinion regarding the means. Some factions believed that the way to stop VD was to end all sexual "excess." This included masturbation and any intercourse that was not intended to produce offspring.

Other members of the Social Hygiene Movement wanted to eliminate VD through sex education, legislation, improved medical care, and access to birth control. They were constantly battling with members who felt birth control would only encourage illicit sexual activities and spread disease.

In addition, although it was increasingly obvious that many women were being infected by their husbands, sex and venereal disease remained taboo subjects. In 1906, the *Ladies Home Journal* ran an editorial about VD. Thousands of women reacted by canceling their subscriptions.

The medical community was also divided concerning methods of dealing with VD. At about the same time the *Ladies Home Journal* incident occurred, Dr. P. S. Pelouze presented a scientific paper about gonorrhea at a medical conference in the United States. The negative reaction from his colleagues was astounding. The following account of what happened can be found in "Venereal Disease Control by Health Departments in the Past: Lessons for the Present," which appeared in the April 1988 issue of the *American Journal of Public Health.* One of Pelouze's colleagues told him:

"Pelouze, you are making a grave mistake in letting yourself become known as one interested in gonorrhea; it will ruin you."

Pelouze replied, "Do you mean that a doctor who shows an interest in a disease that afflicts millions of human beings and has been so badly neglected by our profession that our lack of knowledge upon it is our greatest medical blot will be ruined?" The colleague replied, "Most assuredly."

"Don't you think then," said Pelouze, "that it is time a few of us were ruined?"

ADVANCES OF THE TWENTIETH CENTURY

In the first 10 years of the 20th century, three crucial advances in the diagnosis and treatment of syphilis occurred. In 1905, German scientists Fritz Schaudinn and Eric Hoffmann identified the microorganism that caused the disease. The very next year, August Wassermann and his colleagues developed the *Wassermann test,* the first to allow doctors to determine whether this microorganism was present in the patient's bloodstream.

In 1909 scientist Paul Ehrlich and his assistant, Sahachiro Hata, developed Salvarsan, the first effective treatment for syphilis. Ehrlich and his associates began to concoct different arsenic-type drugs and used rabbits to test the effectiveness of the mixtures against syphilis. In the 606th experiment, the researchers discovered the compound they needed. Tests on humans confirmed the drug's effectiveness, and

In 1909, scientist Paul Ehrlich developed Salvarsan, the first truly effective cure for syphilis.

doctors immediately began injecting their syphilitic patients. Salvarsan was nicknamed "the magic bullet," and although the earliest batches often proved to be highly toxic, refinements were quickly made. Salvarsan treatment, which usually lasted 18 months, became standard therapy until the development of modern antibiotics. Ehrlich won a Nobel Prize for his accomplishment.

Treatment Versus Morality

The introduction of Salvarsan was met with mixed reactions. Many people, even doctors, were concerned that a cure for venereal disease would only encourage "immoral" behavior. Howard Kelly, a member of the extremely prestigious Johns Hopkins medical faculty, was one of the many critics. His reaction to Salvarsan is reported in Allan Brandt's book *No Magic Bullet,* published by Oxford University Press in 1987: "I believe that if we could in an instant eradicate the [venereal] diseases, we would also forget at once the moral side of the question, and would then, in one short generation, fall wholly under the domination of the animal passions, becoming grossly and universally immoral."

This sentiment was widespread among the public, which largely believed that venereal disease was proper punishment for what was considered to be improper sexual behavior. Often victims of STDs were publicly humiliated or punished. In Scotland in the 15th century, people with VD were branded on the face with a hot iron. In St. Louis, Missouri, in the 1870s, infected prostitutes were quarantined in a Social Evil Hospital.

Although it is difficult to imagine today, in 1936 Surgeon General Thomas Parran was prevented from using the word *syphilis* in a radio broadcast. It was still thought that "nice people did not get syphilis," or at least they did not talk about it. In the face of such pressure, it is no wonder that many people suffered in silence and failed to seek treatment.

Fortunately, in the second half of the 20th century, public attitudes changed regarding patients with STDs. This was a result of a combination of factors, including the women's movement, sex education, the advancement of medicine, and new attitudes toward sexuality. Unfortunately, this tolerance is not always extended to people infected with AIDS, the most recently identified STD.

The War Years

By the time the United States entered World War I, nine states had passed legislation requiring doctors to report STD cases to their state government. This allowed state health officials to monitor the spread of these illnesses, a particularly important issue considering that venereal disease had already become the most common reason young men failed their army physicals. Although the number of cases in Europe at this time can only be estimated, it is thought that in some large European cities more than 50% of the adult population had syphilis during the war years. The rapid spread of venereal disease is believed to have seriously compromised the Allies' military ability. As a result, American soldiers were forbidden to seek out prostitutes, and those who became infected with VD were punished. By the end of World War I, 46 states had adopted policies of mandatory reporting and free treatment.

During the late 1920s and early 1930s, Surgeon General Parran instituted a national public health program to eliminate venereal disease.

Funded with federal money, the program included training in VD treatment, funding for diagnostic and treatment facilities, and development of public education programs.

Between the wars, however, interest in VD fell, but the disease regained public attention with the outbreak of World War II. Again, a very high percentage of potential recruits were rejected because of syphilis. Fortunately, just days before the Japanese bombing of Pearl Harbor, a major advance occurred in the treatment of VD. Dr. John Mahoney, an American physician, injected penicillin, the wonder drug discovered in 1929, into four men with syphilis. Within days, three of the men had negative Wassermann tests. Finally, a rapid cure was possible.

The effectiveness of penicillin, combined with easy access to treatment, virtually eliminated VD in the United States. A few years after the war ended, public VD clinics began closing for lack of patients. It became rare for a medical student to see a syphilitic sore or rash.

In 1929, Alexander Fleming (left) discovered penicillin. Twelve years later, Dr. John Mahoney found that the drug could cure syphilis, and for a time the disease was almost eliminated in the United States.

THE CURRENT EPIDEMIC

Unfortunately, VD did not stay away. By the early 1960s, it became obvious that syphilis and gonorrhea were back and threatening to spread out of control. A rapidly increasing number of patients were seeking treatment for STDs, and newborn babies with syphilis were showing up in hospital delivery rooms. New strains of gonorrhea that were not responding to treatment with penicillin were being reported for the first time. Both familiar STDs and new varieties were being identified in patients throughout the United States.

The new STD explosion was the result of many changes occurring at about the same time. These changes began in the 1960s and continued through the 1980s, dramatically affecting the American lifestyle. Availability of birth control pills, an increase in leisure time, the ability to travel farther and faster, the increasingly younger age at which people became sexually active, the availability of multiple sexual partners, and the increasing abuse of alcohol and drugs are the changes most often mentioned.

The United States is still combating an STD epidemic, but this time, with the incurable and fatal addition of AIDS, the stakes are higher than ever. If the fight against STDs is to be won, information, prevention, and treatment must again become top priorities.

3

TRANSMISSION AND DETECTION

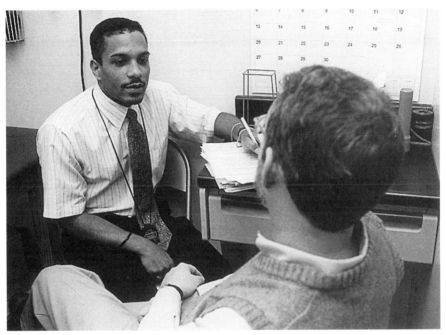

To avoid serious complications, anyone who suspects that he or she is suffering from venereal disease should seek immediate diagnosis and treatment at a doctor's office or a clinic.

S exually transmitted diseases occur more commonly than any other category of infectious disease in the United States. According to studies by national health organizations, more than 12 million new cases of STDs occur each year in the United States, and at least 3 million of them occur in teenagers. Transmission of most STDs requires direct exposure to infected tissue, blood, semen, or vaginal secretions.

Sexual habits and preferences determine which areas of the body are most likely to be exposed to STDs. As would be expected, the *genitalia,* or genital organs, are the most frequent sites of infection. Knowing the anatomy of these organs offers insight into how STDs invade the body and how they spread once exposure occurs. For individuals who engage in oral or anal sex, the mouth, throat, or anus are also frequent sites for exposure and transmission.

FEMALE GENITAL ORGANS

External

The external genital structures of females are often grouped together and referred to as the *vulva.* Included in this group are the *mons pubis, clitoris, labia majora, labia minora, vestibule, urethra, hymen, Bartholin's glands, Skene's glands, fourchette,* and *perineum.* Each of these organs has a unique function. The mons pubis is a pad of fat that protects the pubic bone. It is generally underdeveloped in very young girls and in women who have completed menopause. It is thickest and fullest during the reproductive years. Early students of anatomy recognized this change and referred to the mons pubis as the *mons veneris,* naming it after the Roman love goddess.

The labia majora, also known as the large lips of the vagina, are thick folds of fatty tissue that develop at puberty. They extend from the mons pubis and enclose and protect the genitalia. The labia majora contain large *sebaceous glands* that secrete lubricating fluids. The outer surface of the labia majora is generally covered with pubic hair, and the inner surface is smooth and moist. Even a microscopic abrasion in this area makes it a likely target for STD exposure.

Within the labia majora lie a second pair of lips or folds of skin. These are the labia minora. Smaller and thinner than the labia majora, the labia minora extend vertically from the clitoris and surround the opening to the vagina. At the base of the vulva, the labia majora and the labia minora rejoin. Here the four lips form a juncture called the fourchette.

The *clitoris* is a small organ that protrudes beneath the mons pubis. One fold of the labia minora envelops it from the top; the other fold covers the bottom. The clitoris is similar to the penis in many respects.

It contains erectile tissue that, when stimulated, swells as the tissue fills with blood.

Within the labia minora and between the clitoris and the fourchette lies an oval area known as the vestibule. Within it is found the urethra, a small tubular structure that connects to the bladder and allows urine to be eliminated from the body. It is lined with a thin, moist membrane and in females is very short. During sexual intercourse, infectious agents such as the bacteria that causes gonorrhea can readily come into contact with the urethra and penetrate its delicate lining, causing a venereal infection.

The vestibule also contains lubricating glands. These include Skene's glands, located close to the urethra, and Bartholin's glands, which lie

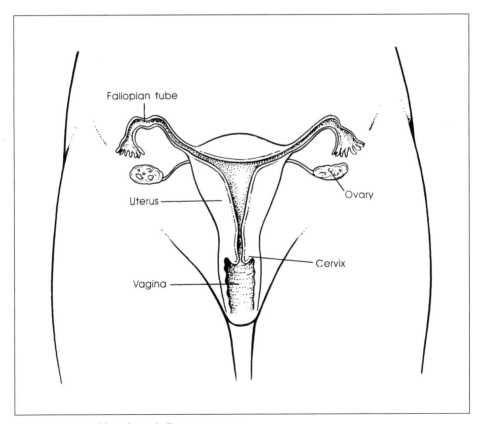

Figure 1: *Internal female genitalia*

near the opening of the vagina. These glands can provide an additional passageway into the body for gonorrhea and other STDs.

Most women who have never experienced sexual intercourse will have a thin ring of tissue stretched across the opening of the vagina. This is called the *hymen*. It can be torn by strenuous physical activity, including sexual activity. Many women who still have a hymen in place at the time of their first sexual penetration will experience minor bleeding and slight pain as the hymen is torn. The region of tissue and muscle that keep the vagina and the rectum apart is called the perineum.

Internal

Internal female genitalia include the vagina, *cervix, fallopian tubes,* and *ovaries*. The vagina is tubular and muscular and is lined with mucous membranes. It connects the *uterus* to the vestibule and is usually less than four inches long. The vagina allows sperm to reach the fallopian tubes and is the pathway through which menstrual blood is eliminated from the body. During normal childbirth, the vagina stretches to accommodate the passage of the baby from the mother's body.

The uterus is a pear-shaped organ that is connected at its upper end to the fallopian tubes. At the lower end, the uterus narrows into a firm necklike structure known as the cervix. The cervix ends in a dimpled opening that extends into the vagina.

The primary function of the uterus is to hold and nourish the fetus during pregnancy. For pregnancy to occur, however, a mature egg must come in contact with a live sperm cell; this is the job of the fallopian tubes. One of these narrow, hollow tubes can be found extending from each side of the uterus, close to its top.

Fallopian tubes measure approximately four inches in length and terminate near the ovaries. The part of the tube closest to the ovary ends in numerous fingerlike projections that reach out like thin strands of hair to propel the mature egg toward the uterus and to provide assistance to the approaching sperm. Fertilization most often occurs in the fallopian tubes. The fertilized egg is then transported to the uterus.

The ovaries are almond-shaped organs, and one lies on each side of the uterus. A normal female is born with more than 400,000 imma-

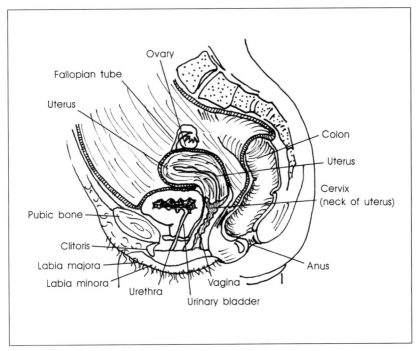

Figure 2: *Internal female genitalia (cross section)*

ture eggs already inside her ovaries. One of these eggs will mature each month from the time a woman begins menstruation until she completes menopause. The ovaries are also an important source of female sexual hormones.

As a result of vaginal sexual intercourse, sperm is released into the vagina. From there it travels through the cervix, into the uterus, and out to the fallopian tubes. This means that if a male partner is infected with an STD, his semen may transmit the infection to any or all of the organs along this route. Infections may also spread if unrecognized and untreated. It is not at all uncommon for a woman to have syphilis lesions on her cervix without the warning symptom of pain. Gonorrhea in women can also be difficult to detect because noticeable symptoms do not appear early. As a result, many women do not realize they have been exposed to an STD and do not seek treatment. This places them at risk of becoming permanently sterile as infection spreads through internal genital organs to the fallopian tubes.

MALE GENITAL ORGANS

External

The external sex organs of males are the *penis* and *testes.* Unless stimulated, the penis usually lies slackly between the legs. Within the penis are three cylinders of tissue that become engorged with blood during periods of sexual excitation. The swelling of these tissues causes the penis to become erect.

The tip of the penis is called the *glans penis.* It is covered with a mucous membrane and is tightly packed with nerve endings. In men who have not been circumcised, the head of the penis is covered by a protective tissue known as *the foreskin.* During erection, the foreskin automatically retracts, exposing the glans penis to direct stimulation. It is this stimulation that results in orgasm and ejaculation.

To date, studies have failed to show conclusively that circumcision either increases or decreases the level of sexual sensation. Although many doctors feel that the foreskin offers valuable protection to the glans penis, studies indicate that circumcision may offer important health benefits by reducing the incidence of urinary tract infections, STDs, and cancer of the penis. The American Academy of Pediatrics states that there are potential benfits and advantages as well as disadvantages and risks. The Academy recommends that accurate and unbiased information about the benefits and risks be provided to the parents, who should then determine what is in the best interest of the child.

Although the skin covering the external male genitalia is less delicate than the membranes found internally, even a microscopic abrasion can provide entry for an STD. In men, the appearance of specific types of ulcers or sores on the penis indicates the exact site of exposure. In women, the exposure area can be much more difficult to determine since the site is often on an internal portion of the genitalia.

The urethra in males opens at the head of the penis and allows for both the ejaculation of semen and the passage of urine. It is approximately eight inches in length, making it about twice as long as the fe-

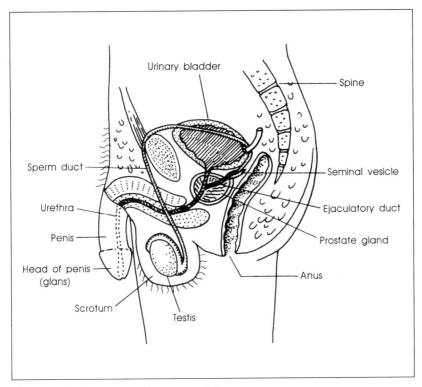

Urinary bladder

Spine

Sperm duct

Seminal vesicle

Urethra

Ejaculatory duct

Penis

Prostate gland

Head of penis
(glans)

Anus

Scrotum

Testis

Figure 3: *Male external and internal genitalia*

male urethra. In males, the tube travels from the head, along the base of the penis, through the *prostate gland,* and connects to the bladder. As with females, Skene's glands lubricate the urethra.

The testes are round, glandular organs that produce sperm and hormones. They are located within the *scrotum,* a pouch of skin that lies beneath the penis. Each of the two testes has a duct known as a *vas deferens* that transports mature sperm to the urethra.

Internal

The vase deferentia (the plural term for the duct) are both external and internal structures. They begin at the testes and progress internally, connecting with the *seminal vesicles* before emptying into the urethra.

The seminal vesicles are small pouches that add a nutrient-rich solution to the sperm as they are transported from the testes. More liquid secretions are produced by the prostate, a small, dense gland that is similar in both size and shape to a chestnut. It lies below the bladder and surrounds the urethra. During ejaculation, 20 or 30 tiny ducts leading directly from the prostate pour secretions into the urethra. The mixture of sperm and liquid is called *semen*.

The internal organs and ducts of the male genitalia are lined with delicate, thin, moist membranes, just as female genitalia are, and are also easily infected. The urethra, which transports both urine and semen, is a frequent conduit for STDs. This permits infections to reach the testes, seminal vesicles, prostate gland, and genital glands and ducts.

STD EXAMINATION

As with most diseases, STDs respond best to early diagnosis and treatment. In the chapters that follow, detailed descriptions of the most common STDs will be provided along with their symptoms. Anyone experiencing such symptoms, or who otherwise has reason to believe that he or she may be infected, should avoid sexual contact and visit a doctor or an STD clinic as soon as possible. Often STDs do not cause noticeable symptoms, particularly in the early phases of infection.

Most doctors recommend annual STD examinations for anyone who is sexually active. It is important to answer the doctor's questions thoroughly. That means not only reporting any signs or symptoms of disease but also providing a complete description of all intimate contact.

The Female Exam

The patient generally lies on her back on the examining table with her feet resting above in stirrups. The physician will begin by examining the external genitalia and surrounding area for signs of infection. In order to examine the vagina and cervix, the doctor will insert a duck-billed instrument known as a *speculum* into the vagina. Once the speculum is in place, the doctor can look for ulcers or unusual discharge or detect whether abnormal odors, unusual redness of the skin, or other symptoms of infection are present.

Most doctors recommend that all women over the age of 21 as well as younger women who are sexually active have an annual *Pap smear.* This test is extremely effective for diagnosing cancer of the cervix and detecting precancerous changes in the cells. The procedure, which takes place during the internal exam, involves removing a small sample of cells from the surface of the cervix. The samples are then sent to a laboratory for analysis.

Following the internal examination, the physician may perform a *bimanual exam* of the pelvic organs, in which he or she will use the hands to feel for any lumps or unusual enlargements in the uterus and ovaries. The buttocks will then be separated, and the area surrounding the anus will be examined.

Although many women feel uneasy during this examination, it should not be a painful experience. Some women feel more comfortable if a female physician performs the procedure. Routine examinations can also be performed by nurse practitioners who have received special training.

The Male Exam

This exam is most often performed with the patient standing. The physician will begin by visually examining the external genitalia and surrounding area. As the penis is inspected, special attention will be given to the urethra and scrotum for evidence of infection, swelling, or soreness. If the patient is not circumcised, the doctor will pull back the foreskin to examine the glans penis and underside of the foreskin. The penis will be massaged either by the doctor or the patient to see if any discharge is present. It will be examined for the presence of any rashes, ulcers, or lesions. The examination will also include a careful inspection of the anus and surrounding area.

Laboratory Tests

On the basis of both the interview with the patient and the physical examination, the doctor will determine which, if any, laboratory tests for STDs should be performed. If necessary, blood will be drawn. Vaginal, urethral, and penile discharges may also be analyzed, as well as specimens taken from any ulcers or lesions.

4

SYPHILIS AND GONORRHEA

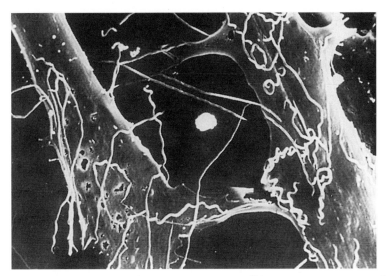

Microscopic view of the syphilis bacterium Treponema pallidum. *Over 100,000 cases of sexually transmitted syphilis occur each year in the United States. In addition, over 3,000 newborns acquire syphilis from their mothers before or during birth.*

SYPHILIS

Before penicillin became widely available, syphilis was the most commonly reported STD in the United States. In the early 1940s, approximately 73 out of every 100,000 people had the disease. Ten years later, this figure dropped to less than 4 in 100,000. In recent decades, the incidence of syphilis has reflected changes in sexual attitudes. During the 1960s and 1970s, syphilis increased as sexual morals became more liberal. It was particularly widespread among the male homosexual community. By the mid-1980s, however, the knowledge that the AIDS virus was spread through sexual activity caused many people to change their behavior. This was particularly true of gay men. As a result, the incidence of syphilis showed a significiant decline.

Unfortunately, the heterosexual community was less inclined to modify its sexual behavior. As a result, the number of people with syphilis again climbed at an alarming rate. In 1997, experts from the National Institute of Allergy and Infectious Diseases (NIAID) estimated that more than 100,000 new cases of syphilis occurred, most of which went undetected by the infected person. The disease is increasing most rapidly among heterosexuals between the ages of 15 and 39 who live in urban areas. The number of infants infected with syphilis at birth is also increasing.

A 1997 report from the Centers for Disease Control (CDC) indicates that there has been a significant increase in the number of syphilis cases in the inner cities among drug users, prostitutes, and the customers of these prostitutes. A large portion of the problem has been traced to the epidemic of crack-cocaine use, because addicted prostitutes often trade sex for drugs. Focused programs of control and prevention appear to be reducing the incidence of syphilis.

Symptoms and Stages

Syphilis is caused by a bacterium called Treponema pallidum, one of a group of corkscrew-shaped microorganisms known as *spirochetes.* The disease is usually transmitted through direct contact with a lesion or sore on an infected sexual partner. The mucous membranes lining the genitals, the mouth, and the anus provide an ideal environment for the syphilis bacteria to thrive. They can also enter the body at any point at which the skin is broken. In addition, pregnant women can transmit the infection to their unborn children.

If untreated, the disease will progress through at least three stages: *primary, secondary,* and *latent.* A fourth stage, known as the *late stage,* will occur in approximately one-third of all untreated cases. Late-stage syphilis is usually accompanied by severe and irreversible complications.

Primary Syphilis   The first symptom of primary syphilis generally occurs approximately three weeks after exposure to the disease. A small, usually painless bump called a *chancre* (pronounced shang'ker) will erupt at the point of entry. Sometimes more than one chancre will appear. They are most often found on the genitals, although they can also appear on the lips, tongue, anus, nipples, tonsils, eyelids, and fingers. Because they are painless and tend to develop on the female internal organs, chancres often go unnoticed in women.

At first, the chancre appears as a hard red pimple. Slowly, its top layer erodes, the chancre begins to spread, and a moist, clear base forms surrounded by hard, raised edges. At this point, the chancre looks like a rounded ulcer with clearly marked borders. It is extremely contagious. During the primary stage, lymph glands near the site of infection can become swollen. Glands in the groin and throat are most often affected.

Secondary Syphilis With or without treatment, the chancre will usually vanish in three to six weeks. This does not mean, however, that the disease has disappeared. Without proper treatment, syphilis will progress into the secondary stage, commonly within 2 to 12 weeks after the chancre is gone.

A skin rash usually signals the beginning of stage two. It can spread over the entire body or show up in just a few areas, such as the palms, the soles of the feet, the chest, the back, the face, or the scalp. If another person touches this rash, he or she may also become infected.

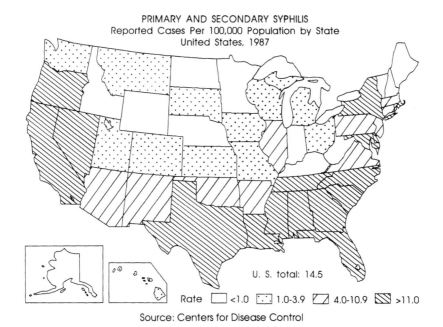

PRIMARY AND SECONDARY SYPHILIS
Reported Cases Per 100,000 Population by State
United States, 1987

U. S. total: 14.5

Rate [ ] <1.0 [∴] 1.0-3.9 [⁄] 4.0-10.9 [⧄] >11.0

Source: Centers for Disease Control

Ancient Inca statue showing syphilis lesions.

In warm, moist areas such as the perineum, scrotum, and vulva, as well as under the arms and between layers of fat, the rash can flourish into large masses of pink or gray lesions. These are called *condyloma lata* and are extremely infectious.

Flulike symptoms are also common during the secondary stage. These can include mild fever, fatigue, headache, swollen lymph glands, sore throat, weight loss, and nausea.

Diagnosing syphilis from symptoms in the secondary stage can be difficult. Because many symptoms are common to other ailments, syphilis is often called the "great imitator." Rashes caused by syphilis are readily confused with allergic reactions or other skin problems. The flulike symptoms are, as one would expect, often attributed to influenza. Also, secondary symptoms are frequently mild and easy to ignore, so that as a result, a patient may not seek medical help. Secondary syphilis can last as long as two years.

Latent Infection   Once secondary symptoms have disappeared, there is a period of *latent infection*. This means that no new symptoms occur but the disease is still present. Without the presence of rashes or lesions, people with latent syphilis are not contagious. Because it is possible for this stage to last 20 to 40 years, approximately two-thirds of people with untreated syphilis remain latent until their death. For the remaining one-third, the disease will progress into its most destructive and final stage.

Late Syphilis   The last stage of syphilis can result in serious damage to the victim's internal organs and structures. The disease can attack any organ, including the heart, brain, and liver. Bone degeneration also frequently occurs. Late-stage syphilis can result in an inability to walk, loss of bladder control, severe numbness, blindness, insanity, and death, although some late-stage victims are able to survive for a decade or longer. Despite severe illness, victims in this stage of syphilis are usually not infectious.

Syphilis and Pregnancy

Women who are infected with syphilis or become infected during their pregnancy—even mothers in the latent stage of syphilis—can pass the disease on to their unborn child. This is known as *prenatal syphilis*. More than half of the babies infected with syphilis die before or shortly after birth. Of those who survive, many are born blind or with other serious birth defects. Mental retardation, lesions, brain infections, and deformities are common. If the mother seeks treatment for syphilis during her pregnancy, both she and her unborn baby can be cured. If the fetus has already suffered damage, however, it cannot be reversed.

Diagnosis

There are two types of tests used to prove a diagnosis of syphilis. Blood tests are used to initially screen the patient for the disease. The Venereal Disease Research Laboratory (VDRL) test, and the *rapid plasma reagin* (RPR) test are two of the most common. They detect whether the body is producing antibodies (disease-fighting proteins) in response to the invasion of syphilis bacteria. Although these tests are fairly accurate within the first few weeks after a chancre has appeared, they are most effective during the secondary stage. However, there is a tendency for certain groups of people to test positive for syphilis even when they are not infected. Drug addicts, pregnant women, and people suffering from diseases of the immune system are among these groups.

Following a blood test, a *dark field microscopic examination* can be used to confirm the diagnosis. The test is named after the type of microscope used to perform it. To carry out this test, a doctor scrapes a small sample of tissue from a lesion. If the bacteria are present, they will appear under the microscope and an immediate diagnosis can be made.

A particularly accurate blood test for syphilis, and one that can be used during any stage of infection, is the *fluorescent treponemal antibody* (FTA) test. This measures the presence of identifiable components of the syphilis bacteria. Once people have been exposed to syphilis, however, their blood usually reacts positively on this test for the rest of their life, even after the disease has been cured. For this reason, the FTA

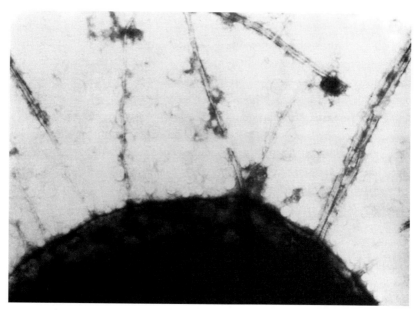

Microscopic view of the gonorrhea bacterium. Approximately 800,000 new cases of gonorrhea are reported in the United States each year.

test is not used for follow-up testing. Usually, the VDRL test is used to make sure that treatment has been effective.

Treatment

In the early stage of syphilis infection, one injection of penicillin will usually be aufficient to cure the patient. Several injections spread out over three weeks may be necessary if the patient has been infected for a long time. The sexual partner or partners of anyone diagnosed with syphilis should also seek diagnosis and treatment immediately, even if they have no symptoms. On average, one out of every two people who have intimate contact with someone suffering from a contagious stage of syphilis will also get the disease.

For people allergic to penicillin, other antibiotics are available for treatment. Usually, patients with syphilis are no longer contagious 24 hours after they begin treatment. People should not, however, return to sexual activities until they have had at least one follow-up blood test that is negative. Syphilis can be cured in all stages. However, the damage done to organs in late-stage syphilis cannot be reversed.

GONORRHEA

Galen, a Greek physician who lived during the second century B.C. is credited with naming the disease known as gonorrhea. In Latin, *gonorrhea* means "flow of seed." Although Galen correctly noted that infected men often suffer a discharge from their penis, he mistakenly assumed that this discharge was semen. He was also wrong in believing that only men could contract this disease. Modern science knows a great deal more about gonorrhea, but unfortunately this knowledge has not been sufficient to eliminate it.

Approximately 800,000 new cases of gonorrhea occur each year in the United States, and public health experts estimate that an additional million gonorrhea infections go unreported each year. Although these numbers seem very large, the disease occurs less frequently now than it did in the 1980s. The rate of infection among young unmarried people between the ages of 15 and 24, however, remains very high. Study results released in 1997 by the Institute of Medicine estimate that $1.1 billion is now being spent each year in the United States for the diagnosis and treatment of gonorrhea.

Transmission

Like syphilis, gonorrhea is also caused by bacteria. In the case of gonorrhea, the infective agent is *Neisseria gonococcus,* a microorganism identified in 1879, more than 25 years before the syphilis bacterium was discovered.

Gonorrhea is almost always spread through sexual activity involving direct contact with mucous membranes. It is readily transmitted through vaginal, anal, or oral intercourse. The cervix, the urinary tract, the mouth, and the rectum provide ideal points of entry for the disease. In women, the most common site of infection is the cervix. In men, it is the urethra. Although the infection can be spread from a man's penis to the throat of his sex partner, it is much less likely that a man will contract or spread the disease by performing oral sex on a female partner.

Gonorrhea can also be passed from a mother to her baby during childbirth. The greatest danger for the newborn is blindness, but this can be prevented by placing a few drops of silver nitrate in the child's eyes immediately after delivery. Because this treatment is so safe and effective, it has become standard procedure for all babies born in hospitals throughout the United States. Children who are infected with

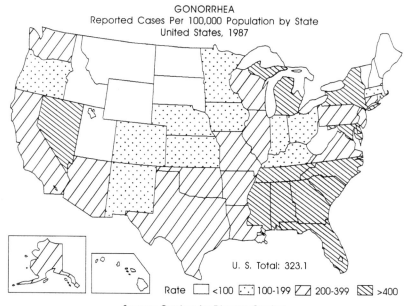

GONORRHEA
Reported Cases Per 100,000 Population by State
United States, 1987

U. S. Total: 323.1

Rate ☐ <100 ⬚ 100-199 ▨ 200-399 ▧ >400

Source: Centers for Disease Control

gonorrhea during birth can be cured and, if treated early, rarely suffer any effects from the disease.

Symptoms

One reason that gonorrhea continues to occur in epidemic numbers is that it is not always easy to detect. Symptoms usually develop within a week or two following exposure but can be very weak and, in many cases, easily overlooked.

It is estimated that among women infected with gonorrhea, fewer than 20% experience noticeable symptoms until more serious complications develop, although these women will be able to transmit the disease before symptoms appear. The most common signs of gonorrhea are inflammation of the cervix and secretion of a white or yellow discharge. If the bacteria have invaded the urethra, urination may become painful as well as more frequent. If allowed to progress untreated, the infection can cause arthritis and blood infection. In addition, it is one of the primary causes of *pelvic inflammatory disease* (PID), the symptoms of which include fever, chills, and abdominal and back pain. PID frequently results in permanent sterility.

Gonorrhea is somewhat simpler to detect in men. Early symptoms will be extremely noticeable about 80% of the time and generally occur within 1 week from the time of exposure. The most common are a burning sensation during urination, a white or yellowish discharge from the penis, and soreness and swelling at the opening of the urethra. Both men and women who contract gonorrhea through anal intercourse may experience inflammation of the anus, painful bowel movements, and a puslike discharge.

Diagnosis and Treatment

A diagnosis of gonorrhea can be confirmed through either a *culture test* or a *Gram's stain test*. Frequently, both are used. The culture test is performed with a sample of the discharge taken from the cervix, urethra, anus, or throat, depending on the site of infection. The sample is allowed to incubate for at least two days and is then examined for the presence of gonorrhea bacteria. In contrast, the Gram's stain test provides faster results but is less accurate in diagnosing gonorrhea in women. Using this test, a sample of the discharge is applied to a slide treated with a special dye. If the gonorrhea bacteria are present, they will show up under microscopic examination approximately 90%–95% of the time in males with symptoms and 50%–70% of the time in men

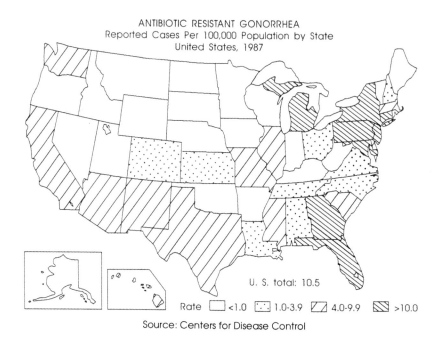

ANTIBIOTIC RESISTANT GONORRHEA
Reported Cases Per 100,000 Population by State
United States, 1987

U. S. total: 10.5

Rate ☐ <1.0 ☐ 1.0-3.9 ☐ 4.0-9.9 ☐ >10.0

Source: Centers for Disease Control

without symptoms. In women, however, the test will find bacteria only 50%–70% of the time whether the patient has symptoms or not.

Gonorrhea frequently occurs in combination with other STDs (possibly because gonorrhea may reduce a patient's resistance to other diseases). By far the most frequent one is chlamydia (see Chapter 6). Gonorrhea and syphilis also occur together fairly frequently. Most doctors and public health professionals routinely test for all three diseases whenever there is reason to suspect exposure to any one of them.

Gonorrhea can be treated with antibiotics either by injection or with pills. Because penicillin-resistant gonorrhea is common, other antibiotics are used. Ceftriaxone, which the doctor can inject in a single dose, is very effective. Other antibiotics, which can be taken orally, include cefixime, ciprofloxacin, and ofloxacin. Since gonorrhea frequently occurs with chlamydia, doctors usually prescribe a combination of antibiotics, such as ceftriaxone and doxycycline. Sexual partners of people diagnosed with gonorrhea should also be tested and treated even if they show no symptoms. After treatment has been completed, a follow-up test infection is gone. Research continues to try to develop a vaccine for gonorrhea.

GENITAL LESIONS

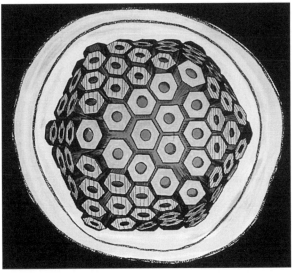

Electron micrograph drawing of a herpesvirus; an estimated 500,000 new cases of genital herpes occur annually.

The characteristic chancre of early-stage syphilis is just one of many skin eruptions that can signal an STD infection. Many other STDs also cause genital lesions, sores, or bumps.

HERPES SIMPLEX

Herpes simplex is an extremely contagious, recurring, and incurable disease. It is caused by a virus that is related to, but different from, the virus that causes chicken pox. The herpes simplex virus has two different forms. *Type 1 is* usually limited to the oral area and shows up as cold sores or fever blisters. *Type 2* produces lesions that are most often confined to the genital area. People who engage in oral sex, however, can spread oral herpes to the genitals and genital herpes to the mouth, lips, and throat.

Reports from the National Institutes of Health (NIH) estimate that 135 million Americans are infected with oral herpes and more than 45 million have genital herpes. Over the last 15 years, the prevelance of oral herpes has remained the same in the United States, while the prevalence of genital herpes has increased 30%. About 1 out of 5 people over the age of 12 is infected with herpes simplex type 2 virus.

Transmission and Symptoms

Unlike flu viruses, herpesvirus dies when exposed to air. This makes it almost impossible to become infected with herpes from contact with toilet seats or other objects. The virus is most often transmitted through direct exposure to active lesions or infected genital secretions.

The initial outbreak or attack of symptoms most often occurs 2 to 20 days following exposure. Small red bumps appear at the site of infection. In women, genital herpes may appear on the external organs of the vulva, within the vagina, or around the anus or buttocks. In men, they most often appear on the penis, anus, buttocks, or scrotum. In a matter of days, the bumps become raised, fluid-filled blisters. These eventually open and become ulcers. In the final stage, new skin forms and the ulcers heal. As blisters and as ulcers, the sores are extremely contagious and usually very painful, expecially for women. The intense discomfort of herpes lesions makes them readily distinguishable from those of syphilis, which are generally painless. In rare cases, however, herpes symptoms are mild enough to ignore.

For most people, the initial outbreak lasts two to three weeks. During this time, many patients also experience a variety of flulike symptoms such as fatigue, headache, muscle aches, and swollen glands. If the lesions involve the urethra, urination can become very painful.

During the first outbreak, herpesvirus travels from nerve endings at the site of infection to clusters of nerve cells at the spinal cord. Here it is kept alive in an inactive state until the next attack. No one is sure what triggers recurrences, but more than 90% of those who suffer an initial attack will have at least one more. Stress, sickness, injury, and fatigue are some of the factors that may stimulate a herpes outbreak. For women, attacks often occur around the time of menstruation. Some people have frequent, highly painful recurrences. Others may experience only one or two and have mild symptoms. Usually,

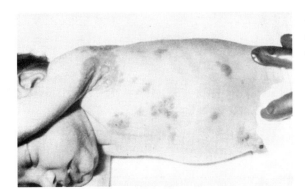

Infant suffering from herpes lesions. Herpes can be passed from an infected mother to her child during birth.

recurrences are not as severe as the original attack. Oral herpes typically recurs less frequently than genital herpes and is often far less painful. Many people with herpes will experience a tingling or itching a few days or perhaps just a few hours before an outbreak occurs. Usually, the sores reappear in the same area as the original attack.

From the time warning signals occur until the lesions are completely healed, the herpes infection is highly contagious. Unprotected oral, anal, or genital sex is extremely risky. Although herpes is most readily spread when a sore is present, researchers now feel that up to 15% of people infected with herpes can transmit the virus during symptom-free periods.

Diagnosis and Treatment

A viral culture provides the most accurate means of distinguishing herpes sores from lesions common to other STDs. Cells are removed from a lesion and added to a sample of healthy cells. If the virus is present, the healthy cells will begin to show signs of herpes infection within two days.

Although there is still no cure for herpes, the antiviral drug acyclovir has been used since 1982 to treat genital herpes. Acyclovir can be used during the initial outbreak as well as during recurrent episodes to limit the length and severity of symptoms. It is administered in pill form and is usually prescribed for a period of a week to 10 days during each episode. People who suffer frequent recurrences can use it daily for up to one year to prevent and control outbreaks.

Complications

Some studies indicate that women infected with genital herpes may have a greater chance of developing cervical cancer. This risk can be minimized if these women receive routine Pap smears to detect any abnormalities in cells of the cervix.

A pregnant woman with active genital herpes is more likely to have a miscarriage or to give birth to a premature or stillborn baby than is a woman who does not carry the infection. In addition, infants born to mothers with infectious herpes lesions can contract the disease while passing through the birth canal. This can be prevented if the baby is delivered through cesarean section—removal through an incision in the mother's abdomen. However, recent studies by the CDC indicate that infection may also occur while the baby is in the womb. Herpes can have serious consequences for a newborn, including blindness, brain damage, or even death. Oral herpes, although not as dangerous, can be spread to infants by kissing them.

For many men and women, a diagnosis of herpes can be frightening news. Although the disease becomes manageable for most people, it is still incurable, and it can affect intimate relationships for many years. Patients who make the best adjustment to the disease are those who find help either from their sexual partner or a support group.

Researchers are working to develop a safe and effective vaccine to prevent genital herpes. They are also investigating additional antiviral drugs capable of finding and destroying the virus in its latent form.

CHANCROID

In tropical portions of Africa, Mexico, Southeast Asia, and Central America, *chancroid* (pronounced shang'kroid) occurs at least as often as syphilis, but it is not just a disease of hot climates. According to the CDC, approximately 3,500 cases are reported in the United States each year. Although this number may seem extremely low compared to the number of people who contract herpes, the incidence of chancroid is increasing, and the cost of diagnosing and treating this disease is over $1 million each year.

Transmission and Symptoms

Chancroid is caused by a bacterium that invades through tears in the skin. The microorganism frequently penetrates abrasions that occur during sexual intercourse. One or more lesions usually appear at the

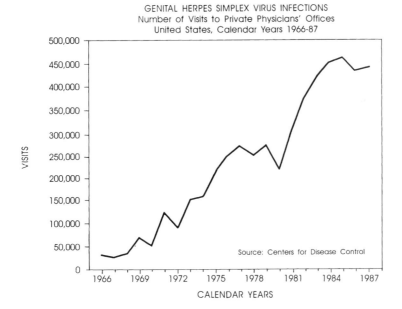

GENITAL HERPES SIMPLEX VIRUS INFECTIONS
Number of Visits to Private Physicians' Offices
United States, Calendar Years 1966-87

Source: Centers for Disease Control

VISITS

CALENDAR YEARS

point of entry within a week after exposure. They can be easily spread by touching a lesion and then touching the genitals.

The chancroid lesion looks like the syphilis chancre. Unlike the syphilis lesion, however, the chancroid chancre is painful. Another important difference is in the texture of the lesions. Whereas the syphilis lesion is most often hard, the chancroid lesion has been accurately nicknamed the "soft chancre." Although women with syphilis frequently have lesions on their cervix, women with chancroid rarely develop cervical lesions.

The chancroid lesion begins as a small red bump. The lesion is usually quite sore and within a few days breaks down and becomes a shallow ulcer with ragged edges. The ulcer can be as small as the head of a pin or measure up to one inch in diameter. It is painful, soft, bleeds easily, produces pus, is often covered with a gray membrane, and can emit a foul odor. Unlike the circular, regular borders of the syphilis chancre, the edges of the chancroid lesion are typically ragged and irregular. Neither syphilis nor chancroid lesions pass through the fluid-filled blister stage characteristic of herpes.

An outbreak of genital chancroid lesions in either men or women is often accompanied by painful swelling of lymph nodes in the groin. Usually, this swelling occurs only on the side of the groin occupied by the lesion. In about half of all untreated chancroid cases these nodes can become severely infected and filled with pus.

Some people, however, can be infected with chancroid and experience no symptoms. Although infants may be infected in the birth canal if the mother is actively infected, chancroid does not appear to be transmitted in the womb.

Diagnosis and Treatment

A physician usually diagnoses chancroid by making a visual examination of the lesions. If necessary, however, a culture test can be performed on the bacteria using cells drawn from the base of a lesion or from pus taken from an infected lymph node.

Chancroid can be successfully treated with antibiotics. Currently, the CDC recommends the use of either erythromycin in pill form for one week or one injection of ceftriaxone. Early treatment of people known to have been exposed to chancroid may prevent the outbreak of lesions.

GENITAL WARTS

The CDC estimates that 1 million new cases of genital warts occur each year in the United States, making this condition the most common STD caused by a virus.

Transmission and Detection

A group of viruses known as *human papillomaviruses,* or HPVs, are responsible for genital warts. They are very similar to the viruses that cause warts on fingers and feet, but genital warts cannot spread to those parts of the body, and vice versa. Genital warts are usually transmitted through sexual intercourse, although in rare instances they can be spread to the mouth through oral sexual contact.

In some cases the warts appear within a few weeks of exposure, but in others, months or years pass before they reach a noticeable size. Even when the warts are too small to see, however, they are highly contagious. Approximately two-thirds of the people exposed to this condition become infected. In men, genital warts are most often found on the tip or shaft of the penis, the scrotum, and the anus. In women, they are likely to develop on the lips of the vagina, within the vagina, in the urethra, on the cervix, or around the anus.

Genital warts are usually painless, although they can cause itching. Sufferers may also experience painful urination if these growths appear within the urethra. The warts are soft to the touch and can either be flat or protrude from the skin in a rough, fleshy nodule that gives them the appearance of tiny cauliflowers. Usually, only one or two warts will appear, but if untreated, they can multiply.

Diagnosis and Complications

Genital warts are most often diagnosed by visual examination. If the warts are very small or (as is frequently the case with cervical warts) of the flat type, the doctor may use a magnifying lens to see them. Moreover, genital warts normally produce no noticeable symptoms, which means that a patient may not seek diagnosis in the first place. If untreated, however, the infection can prove very dangerous. Researchers have found that certain strains of the virus that cause genital warts can play an important role in the development of cervical or vaginal cancer. This is yet another reason for scheduling routine Pap smears. Often an abnormal Pap result provides the first indication of genital warts.

Pregnancy can stimulate genital warts to grow rapidly. If present in the vagina, they can cause blockages and create problems at the time of delivery. A baby exposed to HPV in the birth canal can develop warts on the anus, genitals, or larynx. Although this is not a common event, it can have very serious complications for the newborn infant.

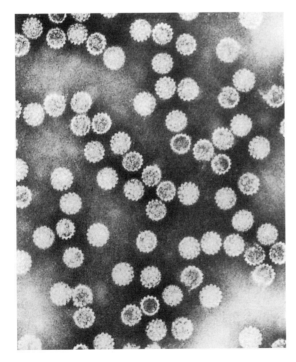

Microscopic view of human papillomavirus, the organism responsible for genital warts.

Treatment

No one should attempt self-treatment of genital warts. Although there are hundreds of different wart potions and salves and even organic remedies on the market, these are not appropriate for genital warts. The skin of the genitals is very sensitive and can be easily damaged by inexpert treatment. In addition, genital warts can be very difficult to spot. Only a trained medical professional can provide a thorough examination and treatment.

Small warts can be removed by freezing them with liquid nitrogen. This technique is known as *cryotherapy*. Warts can also be burned off with a variety of chemical preparations. This treatment usually requires repeated applications and removal of the chemical after each application. Laser surgery is also being used with increasing frequency on genital warts. This therapy utilizes a high-powered light beam to destroy infected tissue. The sooner treatment is begun, the more effective it usually is. Because some warts may be resistant to treatment or may reappear, it is important that patients return for follow-up visits until their doctor indicates they are cured. Patients being treated for genital warts should not engage in intimate sexual contact until the disease is gone.

LESS COMMON STDs

Syphilis, herpes, chancroid, and genital warts account for most of the visible sores, bumps, and lesions that appear on the genitals. There are several other STDs, however, that also produce sores at the site of exposure.

Granuloma Inguinale

Granuloma inguinale, a condition caused by bacteria, is very rare in the United States. Fewer than 100 cases are reported to the CDC each year. The disease is found primarily in tropical countries. The first sign of infection is usually the appearance of small, painless nodules or pimples that enlarge and open into beet red ulcers. Tissue at the base of the ulcer takes on a granulated appearance in which many small, round bumps form. This tissue eventually rises and protrudes above the walls of the ulcer.

These lesions are most often seen on the glans or shaft of the penis in males and on the labia in females. Unlike most other STDs, however, granuloma inguinale is only mildly contagious. Repeated, direct contact with active lesions is thought to be necessary for the infection to spread. Diagnosis can be made either through microscopic identification of the bacteria or by culturing cells from the lesions. If untreated, granuloma inguinale lesions can leave scars. A variety of antibiotics can be used for treatment. Generally these are administered in pill form for three weeks.

Lymphogranuloma Venereum

Lymphogranuloma venereum, also known as LGV, is caused by a strain of the *Chlamydia trachomatis* bacterium, a microorganism that has caused considerable difficulty throughout history. It was discovered in 1907 by scientists examining cells scraped from mucous membranes lining the eyelids of an orangutang with an eye infection. The researchers saw what appeared to be organisms wearing cloaks and named them chlamydia after the Latin word *chlamydatus,* meaning to wear a cloak or mantle.

In the days before modern plumbing, this bacterium was responsible for a great many eye infections among humans. Once standards of personal hygiene improved, however, the problem largely disappeared in developed countries. Today slightly different strains of this bacterium cause either lymphogranuloma venereum or a group of diseases called chlamydia infections (see Chapter 6). Although chlamydia occurs far more often, only LGV must be reported to the CDC. In the United States, fewer than 500 cases of LGV are diagnosed each year. It is seen much more frequently in Southeast Asia.

The first symptom of LGV is usually a small, painless pimple that develops on the genitals within three weeks of exposure. Frequently it will heal and disappear without any treatment, making it very easy to ignore. Unfortunately, this is just the first stage of the disease. If untreated, LGV will usually progress to a second stage, which is characterized by significant swelling of lymph nodes in the affected area. These nodes can become extremely painful, enlarged, filled with pus, and matted together. The swelling can also block normal drainage and cause swelling of external genital tissue as well. If the infection is oral, lymph glands in the throat will be affected. Fever, chills, headache, and weakness may also occur. A diagnosis can be confirmed by drawing pus from a lymph node and examining it for the bacteria. Bacteria-fighting sulfa drugs and tetracycline are both effective in curing this disease.

Molluscum Contagiosum

Although doctors do not have to report cases of *molluscum contagiosum,* disease experts believe that between 200,000 and 300,000 cases are treated each year in the United States. The condition is highly contagious and can be transmitted through sexual activity, although other types of frequent close contact can spread the disease as well. As a result, outbreaks can occur in classrooms, army barracks, and dormitories. The infection usually produces pinkish white, waxy, bubble-like bumps within two to eight weeks of exposure. The bumps are often itchy and appear to have indentations on top. When transmitted through sexual intimacy, the bumps usually appear on the genitals and sometimes on the chest or stomach. Often the lesions are so small that they can be seen only through a magnifying glass.

Diagnosis is usually made by visual examination, although the disease can also be confirmed through a microscopic examination of cells taken from within the lesion. Curing the disease involves eliminating the lesions. Sometimes they will vanish without treatment, but in other cases chemicals, freezing, or electric current can be used by trained medical personnel to speed the healing process and prevent the disease from being transmitted.

SIX COMMON STDs

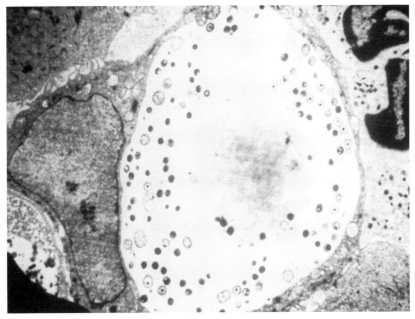

Microscopic view of Chlamydia trachomatis; *each year, approximately 4 mililon people In the United States contract a chlamydla infection.*

D espite the social stigma that remains connected with the term *sexually transmitted disease,* some seemingly minor infections can also be considered STDs. Although at first they may present relatively minor symptoms, these illnesses can result in serious trouble if left untreated.

THE CHLAMYDIA EPIDEMIC

In the previous chapter, different strains of the bacterium *Chlamydia trachomatis* were introduced as the cause of a variety of diseases known collectively as chlamydia infections.

According to estimates from the Centers for Disease Control, approximately 4 million people in the United States contract chlamydia infections each year through intimate contact, and the number is rapidly increasing. Estimated to occur five times as often as gonorrhea and 40 times more frequently than syphilis, chlamydia infections are by far the most common STDs. Males and females between the ages of 15 and 29 make up the largest group of people carrying the disease.

Exposure to chlamydia occurs when mucous membranes come into direct contact with infected semen or vaginal secretions. Vaginal intercourse is the most common cause of transmission, and in women the cervix is the most common site of chlamydia infections. However, the disease can also be spread through oral and anal contact. As a result, chlamydia can infect the throat and anus, causing inflammation, swelling, and discomfort.

Symptoms and Diagnosis

That symptoms are often absent or easy to ignore in the early stages of disease has contributed to the rapid spread of chlamydia. Approximately 80% of women who are infected by the bacteria fail to realize it until they begin to suffer complications as the disease progresses. In some cases, however, the cervix becomes inflamed and produces pus during the early phase of infection. This condition is commonly known as *cervicitis*. The amount of pus formed, however, is so slight that it rarely is noticed among normal vaginal secretions. Cervicitis also commonly results from gonorrhea and herpes, so laboratory tests must be performed to pinpoint the cause. Vaginal bleeding between menstrual periods or after intercourse, painful urination, and lower abdominal pain have also been reported by some women in the early stage of chlamydia infection. Although men are more likely to have early symptoms, they are easily mistaken for symptoms of gonorrhea.

The most common symptom in men infected with chlamydia is inflammation of the urethra. This can cause a burning sensation during urination and the feeling of having to urinate frequently. The penis may also produce a mild discharge. Early symptoms in men generally appear within a week to a month following exposure. The only way to accurately distinguish chlamydia from gonorrhea is to perform a laboratory analysis on a sample of the discharge. Often people infected with gonorrhea are also infected with chlamydia, making an initial diagnosis more difficult. The CDC recommends that treatment for chlamydia be routinely included whenever gonorrhea is treated.

Treatment

Chlamydial infections can be cured with oral antibiotics, usually tetracycline and erythromycin. Treatment generally lasts from 7 to 21 days. The patient should avoid sexual contact until the chlamydia bacteria have been completely eliminated from his or her body.

Transmission to Infants

Approximately half of the infants born to women with chlamydia are infected during birth. These babies frequently develop *conjunctivitis,* an infection of the membrane lining the inner surface of the eye, and can also suffer from pneumonia. However, chlamydia can be treated effectively and safely during pregnancy.

Complications

Although frequently "silent" in its early stages, a chlamydia infection can have widespread and destructive consequences. If untreated, the bacteria can travel up through the reproductive organs, causing chronic and painful infections as well as sterility.

Some of the most common complications of chlamydia are discussed in the pages that follow. Although these conditions can be the result of other microorganisms, chlamydia bacteria are often to blame.

Chlamydia in Men

The narrow tubes that carry mature sperm from the testes to the urethra are known as *epididymes* (and each is known singularly as the epididymis). If chlamydia infections in the urethra are not properly treated, they can spread into these delicate vessels, causing swelling and tenderness near the testicles. The patient may also suffer from a fever. In men under the age of 35, this infection is known as *epididymitis.* There are conflicting reports in medical literature as to whether infertility can result if the infection goes untreated. Fortunately, it responds very well to antibiotics.

Chlamydia in Women

If chlamydia occurs in the cervix and is not treated, the infection can spread to the delicate lining of the uterus, the fallopian tubes, and the ovaries. The result is pelvic inflammatory disease. Chlamydia accounts for 200,000 to 400,000 of the more than 1 million cases of PID diagnosed each year in the United States. PID is also frequently caused by gonorrhea.

Teenagers make up nearly one-fifth of all PID cases, and females who have more than one sexual partner place themselves at particularly high risk. PID can last just a short time if treated early, but if not, the condition can remain for several years. The symptom patients most frequently complain of is pain in the lower abdomen. This may be accompanied by fever, nausea, abnormal vaginal bleeding, pain during sexual intercourse, or unusually long or painful menstrual periods. PID can usually be treated by a combination of antibiotics given in pill form. In some cases, the infection can be severe enough to require hospitalization.

Unfortunately, PID can also occur without producing any noticeable early symptoms. This is frequently the case when it is caused by chlamydia. If allowed to progress untreated, PID can result in long-lasting, or chronic, pelvic pain. It can also cause scarring and blockages in the narrow, delicate fallopian tubes, making it difficult or impossible for mature eggs to pass from the ovaries to the uterus. As a result, chlamydia can render a woman sterile. More than 100,000 women become infertile each year as a result of PID. Recurrent episodes of PID increase a woman's risk of infertility, tubal pregnancy, or chronic pelvic pain. As many as one-third of women who have had PID will have the disease at least once more. Each episode of reinfection increases the risk of infertility.

A doctor can evaluate the damage done by PID through either a *sonogram* or *laparoscopic examination.* A sonogram bounces high-frequency sound waves off of the internal organs to produce a picture of the inner body. In the other test, a small instrument called a *laparoscope* is inserted through a narrow incision in the abdomen to allow visual examination of the fallopian tubes.

In some cases, a woman will become pregnant, but the fertilized egg will become trapped inside a scarred fallopian tube and begin to develop there instead of inside the uterus. This is called *a tubal pregnancy* and is usually accompanied by fever, bleeding, and extreme pain. If the developing egg is not surgically removed, it will burst through the narrow tube, possibly resulting in the woman's death from shock or excessive bleeding.

According to the NIAID, approximately 70,000 ectopic pregnancies occur each year. A large proportion are due to the consequences of PID. Although curing advanced PID can be difficult, progress is being made in preventing it. Rapid, inexpensive, and easy-to-use diagnostic tests are being developed. A recent study found that screening and treating women who unknowingly had chlamydia reduced PID by more than 60%. Studies have also found that vaginal douching may actually encourage the development of PID, perhaps by pushing bacteria into the upper genital tract.

Treatment Options for Infertility

In recent years, great progress has been made in helping women regain the use of damaged fallopian tubes. Through microsurgery, very fine instruments can be used to remove scarred tissue and repair or replace damaged lengths of tube. These procedures, however, are very expensive, and in cases where damage is severe, the success rate is less than 30%. Researchers continue to work on improving the technology and techniques needed to repair damaged tubes.

In vitro fertilization offers an effective alternative for many women by permitting the egg to bypass the fallopian tubes entirely. In this procedure, a mature egg is removed from the patient's ovary, fertilized with sperm, and then returned to the woman's uterus, where it is surgically attached and left to mature.

VAGINITIS

Another common STD is *vaginitis,* a condition that is often transmitted sexually. However, vaginal disease can and does occur in women who are not sexually active as well as in women whose sexual partners are uninfected. Pregnancy, frequent douching, and the use of birth control pills or antibiotics are among the factors that, in some women, can cause changes in the vagina that encourage irritation. The vaginal environment can also be upset by forceful sexual activity; hormonal changes; or use of an IUD, contraceptive foam, or a diaphragm. In addition, underpants made from synthetic material can retain moisture and encourage the development of an infection. (Cotton underpants, which allow air to circulate, are a better choice.)

The three different types of vaginitis diagnosed most commonly are fungal or yeast infections; *trichomoniasis,* an infection caused by single-celled organisms called *protozoa;* and bacterial infections. An accurate diagnosis can usually be made by examining a sample of a vaginal secretion.

YEAST INFECTIONS

Yeast infections, which are caused by a fungus, are the most common type of vaginitis. However, it is not likely to be spread to a woman sexually. The yeastlike fungus responsible for this condition is called *Candida albicans,* and the resulting vaginitis is often known as *candidiasis.*

The primary symptom of a yeast infection is intense vaginal itching. A burning sensation is also common. If an abnormal vaginal discharge occurs, it is usually white and often has the clotted appearance of cottage cheese. In addition, vaginal tissues may become very irritated. Yeast infections most often result from too much lactic acid in the vaginal canal. Doctors can prescribe either pills or medicated vaginal creams to correct the problem. Over-the-counter preparations are also available, which can be purchased without a prescription.

The protozoan organism that causes trichomoniasis is thought to excrete a toxic substance that irritates the vagina.

Women with candida infections can pass them on to their sexual partners. Men who become exposed may suffer a mild infection of the penis and may transmit the disease during intercourse. As a result, women with yeast infections should avoid sexual intercourse until treatment is completed and all symptoms disappear. Infections may need more than one round of treatment.

TRICHOMONIASIS

The protozoa that cause trichomoniasis can thrive in the vagina and are thought to excrete a toxic, irritating substance. This disease is most often spread through sexual intercourse. In both women and men, trichomoniasis can infect the urethra. Infection can also occur through exposure to fingers, douching equipment, and even damp washcloths that have come in contact with infected vaginal secretions. Reports indicate that hot tubs may also provide a means of transmission.

According to the NIAID, each year 3 million men and women in the United States are diagnosed with trichomoniasis. For women, symptoms occur approximately 50% of the time or more. The most common is the production of a thick, usually yellow or gray vaginal discharge that can have an unpleasant odor. Vaginal itching is another frequent symptom, and in fewer cases, discomfort during sexual intercourse and painful urination can also occur. It is very rare for infected men to have any symptoms. Those who do most often experience painful urination or the production of a thin white discharge from the penis.

Trichomoniasis is usually treated with antibiotic pills. If a woman has been diagnosed, she and her sexual partner should be treated even if neither has symptoms. Men can easily infect and reinfect their sexual partner while they have the disease.

BACTERIAL INFECTIONS

Vaginitis can also be caused by an overabundance of bacteria in the vagina. Under normal circumstances, bacteria that live within the vagina play an important role in maintaining female health. From the time a woman enters puberty until she completes menopause, bacteria in her vagina combine with other cells to form lactic acid, which acts as the first line of defense against infection. The ability of the vagina to fend off disease requires that a proper balance of bacteria and lactic acid be maintained.

When the amount of bacteria becomes too great, however, the vagina becomes more susceptible to the infection and inflammation of vaginitis. This condition is also known as *nonspecific vaginitis* and *Gardnerella vaginalis,* named after Dr. Herman Gardner, the first person to recognize that infection could occur when normal bacteria grew out of control. The problem itself is very common and is often transmitted through sexual activity. The most frequent symptom is an abnormal discharge from the vagina, often accompanied by vaginal itching or burning. Sexual intercourse may become painful, and vaginal bleeding may occur following intercourse or between periods.

Once again, infected males rarely have any noticeable symptoms. In women, the most frequent symptom is the production of a vaginal discharge emitting a fishy odor. In some cases, the discharge is yellow or green. Vaginal tissues may appear red and inflamed. Painful intercourse, burning urination, and vaginal itching may occur.

Because this type of vaginitis is caused by bacteria that are normally found in the vagina, there is some disagreement among doctors as to whether the male sexual partner of infected women should also be treated. Usually males are not treated unless the infection of their female sexual partner recurs. The most common treatment is antibiotic pills taken several times a day for a week.

7

AIDS

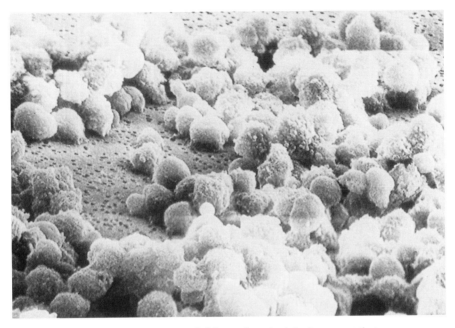

Microscopic view of human immunodeficiency virus, the infectious agent that causes AIDS.

A IDS, or acquired immune deficiency syndrome, is the most deadly and, apparently, the most recent of all sexually transmitted diseases. As mentioned earlier, it is caused by HIV, or human immunodeficiency virus.

EARLY HISTORY OF THE AIDS EPIDEMIC

In the early 1980s, doctors in New York and Los Angeles began to see young, otherwise healthy men showing up in their offices with unusual complaints. Many had dark purple lesions on their body. Upon testing, these lesions were identified as *Kaposi's sarcoma,* a form of skin cancer rarely seen in the United States. At the same time, many young men were suffering bouts of pneumonia that often proved fatal. They seemed to be particularly susceptible to *Pneumocystis carinii,* a type of pneumonia usually seen only in patients whose immune system is destroyed or not functioning. Many of these young men suffered from both skin cancer and pneumonia as well as countless infections, drastic weight loss, fatigue, and fevers of unknown origin.

In comparing cases, doctors began to realize that these men were either homosexuals, drug users who injected their drugs, or both. As the number of cases steadily increased, the physicians realized that a new infectious agent was present and could be transmitted by direct contact with infected blood. In June 1981, the Centers for Disease Control began keeping records on this new contagious disease, which had become known as AIDS.

In 1983, scientists working under the direction of Dr. Robert Gallo in the United States and a research team led by Dr. Luc Montagnier in France simultaneously identified the AIDS virus. This discovery gave people with AIDS as well as professionals in the medical community hope that a cure and a vaccine would soon follow. Unfortunately, neither is available yet, although considerable progress has been made in understanding and treating HIV disease.

According to the CDC, by the end of September 1990 more than 152,000 people in the United States had been diagnosed with AIDS and almost 94,000 of them had died from it. By the end of June 1997, 612,078 people had been diagnosed with AIDS and 379,258 of them had died as a result of the disease.

CRIPPLED IMMUNITY

In order to survive, HIV must invade healthy cells. Once inside, the virus's genetic material is fused with the genetic material of the healthy cell. The virus can then reproduce itself by using the healthy cell as a sort of manufacturing plant. Although HIV has been found in many different types of cells, its primary targets are cells of the immune system, which defend the body against disease.

In the process of replicating themselves, HIV kills off the immune cells it uses. When enough immune cells are destroyed, the body is unable to fight off the countless varieties of infectious microorganisms present in the environment, and the patient becomes much more susceptible to disease.

Researchers have also identified a process in which large numbers of immune cells can be crippled even though they are not infected. As HIV is produced, small particles on the outer surface tend to break off. These particles circulate freely throughout the body and are also highly attracted to the immune cells. Although these particles do not invade healthy cells and do not reproduce, they do attach to immune cells and can make them useless in the fight against invading infections.

PROGRESSION OF THE DISEASE

HIV disease develops very slowly in most people. In the United States, the time between infection with the virus and development of fullblown AIDS is often five to ten years. Several stages of HIV-related

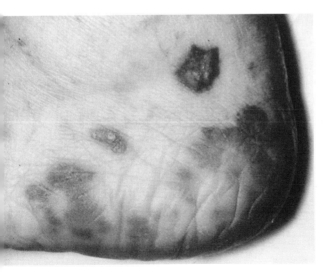

Kaposi's sarcoma on a patient's heel. This form of cancer is normally rare, but crippled immunity makes it common among AIDS patients.

disease have been identified. As more effective treatment becomes available, the ability to determine each specific stage will become even more important.

The initial stage, also known as the period of *primary infection,* occurs shortly after exposure to the virus. Within several weeks following infection most people will develop flulike symptoms. Fever, headache, swollen glands, exhaustion, and sore throat are common. Some people suffer from nausea, diarrhea, and rashes as well. All of these symptoms usually go away without any treatment in one to three weeks.

The second stage can last for years. Most often, people feel quite well. Although the virus has invaded healthy cells, it is either in an inactive stage or is reproducing very slowly.

A significant drop in the number of immune cells is often the first indication that the disease has progressed to the third stage. At this point, the person is susceptible to a wide range of infections and diseases. In the final stage, which is known as AIDS, the immune system has been severely damaged. Most people diagnosed with AIDS die within a couple of years.

Drs. Luc Montagnier (left) and Robert Gallo (right), codiscoverers of the AIDS virus.

TRANSMISSION

HIV can be transmitted by intimate sexual contact or through direct exposure to infected blood, semen, or vaginal secretions. Vaginal intercourse, anal intercourse—and to a lesser extent, oral sex—can transmit the virus. Intravenous drug abusers can spread the virus by sharing needles used to inject drugs. (According to the CDC, of the people diagnosed with AIDS in 1996, 23% of the men and 34% of the women acquired the disease through IV drug use.) Pregnant women can infect their unborn babies in the womb. In several studies, it has been shown that infants can also become infected through nursing if their mother carries the virus in her breast milk.

It has also been discovered that people suffering from syphilis, genital herpes, trichomoniasis, or chancroid are at increased risk of HIV infection because the virus can easily enter the body through genital lesions caused by these diseases. Evidence also indicates that people with gonorrhea, chlamydial infection, or trichonemal infection are at increased risk as well.

Until HIV was identified and a test for the virus became available, many people became infected through blood transfusions. Now all blood banks screen for HIV, and it is almost impossible to receive contaminated blood from a blood bank.

Moreover, the virus cannot be transmitted by an insect bite; by swimming in a pool with an infected person; or by touching a toilet seat, telephone, or towel used by someone infected with HIV. The virus also cannot be transmitted through casual contact, such as shaking hands or hugging. Although HIV has been found in saliva, the CDC knows of no case in which the virus has been spread through "French" kissing.

THE CHANGING AIDS POPULATION

Although homosexual and bisexual men still account for the largest number of reported AIDS cases in the United States, this is rapidly changing. In 1985, this population represented 63% of the people with AIDS. In 1996, however, the percentage of cases known to have been caused through homosexual transmission had dropped to about 50%. This difference reflects an important change in the sexual behavior of gay and bisexual men. As a result of AIDS education programs, many members of this population are engaging in sex with fewer partners and avoiding activities that increase infection risk.

Since testing HIV positive basketball star Magic Johnson has worked to increase aware-ness of AIDS. These Filipino children are getting a lesson in dribbling.

By contrast, the number of children and heterosexual men and women diagnosed with AIDS has increased. From 1988 to 1995, the proportion of AIDS cases in America attributed to heterosexual contact has grown from 4.8% to 17.7%. Almost 11,000 people with AIDS were under age 20 at the time of diagnosis. Of these, over 5,000 have died. In addition, AIDS is now the second leading cause of death in America among people between the ages of 25 to 44.

HIGH-RISK BEHAVIOR

Because someone can be infected with the AIDS virus for many years and not have any symptoms, it can be difficult for a sexually active person to know who is infected. Reducing the chance of infection means eliminating behavior that could result in contact with HIV.

The AIDS Memorial Quilt displayed in Washington DC in 1996 stretched from the Washington Monument to the Capitol. It was created by people from all across the country in memory of loved ones who died from AIDS.

High-risk activities include sharing drug needles with an infected person; having sex with a person who shares needles; having sex with someone who has several sex partners; and participating in anal, vaginal, or oral sex without using a condom.

TESTING AND TREATMENT

To diagnose HIV, a physician does not test the patient's blood for the virus itself but for antibodies produced by the immune system in an attempt to fight off the infection. Although the antibodies do not provide an effective defense against the virus, they do indicate that the body has been invaded by HIV.

The blood test most often used to identify the presence of these antibodies is the *ELISA test.* The ELISA (enzyme-linked immunosorbent assay) is very accurate, easy for trained laboratory personnel to perform, and inexpensive. In most cases, people begin producing antibodies within three months of infection. Because of the seriousness of the disease, if an ELISA test produces a positive response, another ELISA will be run to double-check the results. If the second test is also positive, another type of exam, the *Western Blot test,* will most likely be used to confirm the results.

Although testing for HIV is now very accurate, it is not perfect. There are documented cases, although very few, of people who tested negative for up to three years following infection with HIV. Anyone who tests negative, yet has reason to believe that he or she may have been exposed to the AIDS virus, should be retested every six months for a year or two.

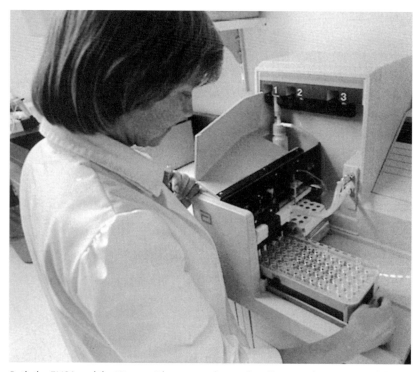

Both the ELISA and the Western Blot test can be used to diagnose the presence of the AIDS virus by detecting antibodies produced to fight the virus.

Confidential testing is available in every state. Further information about testing and HIV infection can be obtained by calling the national toll-free AIDS hot line. A 24-hour information service is available by phoning 800-342-2437.

Although progress is being made, there is still no cure or vaccine for HIV. However, there have been improvements in treatment. *AZT,* which is also called *azidothymidine* or *zidovudine,* was the first antiviral drug that proved effective in slowing down the rate at which the HIV virus reproduces. Other drugs used to treat AIDS include didanosine (dideoxyinosine, ddI), zalcitabine (dideoxcytidine, ddC), and stavudine (deoxythymidine, d4T). These drugs are usually given in combinations of two or more.

To derive the full benefit from care, however, it is crucial for treatment to begin early. Current therapies appear to have the most benefit in the initial stages of infection. By the time people have progressed to

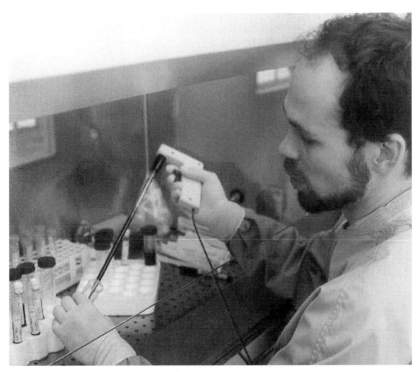

An AIDS researcher from the University of Toronto working with vials of blood in a laboratory.

full-blown AIDS, their immune response is so depleted that it is much more difficult to keep them alive. Many researchers suggest that there will never be one cure for AIDS, but like cancer it will be treated with a variety of drug combinations.

If the virus can be stopped or controlled, HIV infection may someday become a chronic problem, like diabetes, rather than a lethal condition. People with HIV disease would still require fairly regular medical attention, but most could expect to have a relatively normal and healthy life.

The late Ryan White, who contracted AIDS through a blood transfusion, met with public discrimination that for a time prevented him from attending school. In 1984, however, Western High School in Indiana welcomed him as a student.

AIDS IN AFRICA

As devastating as the AIDS epidemic has been to the United States, its impact in Africa has been far worse. It is estimated that over 25 million people there have contracted HIV, and in some cities more than 50% of the adult population is infected, Africa has 70% of the people living with AIDS in the world, 83% of the AIDS deaths worldwide, and 95% of the world's AIDS orphans. The disease has also significantly reduced life expectancy in Africa. Officials from the World Health Organization are urging African nations to declare the AIDS epidemic an emergency.

AIDS has caused chronic overcrowding in many African healthcare facilities. In this hospital in Lilongwe, Malawi patients are lying on the floor because there are no available beds.

PUBLIC REACTION TO AIDS

Although it is now known how to eliminate or minimize risk of exposure to HIV, for people who are already infected the future remains uncertain. These people deserve the care and concern of everyone. In many cases, people with AIDS have suffered discrimination in employment and housing and have been refused insurance benefits. Children with AIDS have been expelled from school, and their families have been shunned by friends and neighbors.

AIDS is everyone's concern and nobody's fault. If not controlled, however, the AIDS epidemic poses a serious threat to the nation's health. Efforts must continue to find effective treatments for HIV disease and to educate people to recognize and avoid high-risk behavior.

8

STD PREVENTION

The decision to become sexually intimate must be made carefully and responsibly in order to reduce the risk of spreading STDs.

Sexual intimacy can be a wonderful experience. It offers pleasure, closeness, and the potential to create new life. Having a sex life that is both satisfying and healthy, however, requires thoughtful decisions. People who behave irresponsibly increase their risk of being exposed to STDs. If infected, some will suffer only minor symptoms; others will face great pain, permanent physical damage, and even loss of life.

PLAY IT SAFE

People who do not have sex or whose only sexual activity is masturbation do not have to worry about STD exposure. Uninfected people who are totally faithful to one sex partner, someone who is also monogamous and who has never had an STD, are also safe. For others, the choice of partners and the choice of sexual activities will determine the level of risk of exposure to STDs.

In general, fewer sex partners means less likelihood of infection. Choosing partners carefully and getting to know a potential lover well before engaging in sex can also reduce the chances of exposure. The better one person knows another, the easier it is to share private thoughts, feelings, and concerns. By talking candidly with a potential sex partner, it may be possible to learn whether he or she is aware of how STDs are spread. It is wise to ask the person whether he or she has ever been infected. Before engaging in intimate contact, it is also a good idea to take a close look at the other person, particularly the partner's genital area. If any sores, rashes, or abnormal discharges are visible, it is best to avoid all direct contact until the person seeks medical attention and treatment is successfully completed.

PRECAUTIONS

Men and women who have sex with more than one partner or have partners who are sexually active with others can take precautions to lower their risk of exposure to STDs. Any sexual activity that involves direct contact with a partner's blood, vaginal secretions, or semen is extremely risky. Activities that are considered very safe include kissing without the exchange of saliva, rubbing against each other while clothed, and touching and massage that does not involve direct contact with exposed genitals.

Condoms

For people who engage in sexual intercourse, condoms provide the best protection. If used properly, they prevent semen from entering or making contact with the vagina. They also protect that portion of the penis covered by the condom from secretions and infectious microorganisms present in the vagina. A condom offers no protection, however, against herpes, genital warts, or other lesions that occur on areas of the penis that the condom does not cover.

In the United States, a variety of condoms are available. Most are made of either latex or lambskin. Although those produced from either material are able to prevent pregnancy, only the latex condoms are considered effective in preventing the transmission of STDs. Preliminary studies have shown that the virus that causes AIDS may penetrate the lambskin varieties.

According to a report in *Fortune* magazine, Americans buy more than a million condoms every day. The use of condoms by sexually active male teenagers between the ages of 15 and 19 has increased dramatically over the past 20 years. In 1979, condom use by this population was approximately 20%. In 1989 it was 57%, and in 1999 it was approximately 70%. Although this figure shows significant improvement, it also indicates that much work is still needed to educate teenagers about disease prevention. Fear of AIDS is the reason given most frequently for the use of condoms.

Although condoms certainly decrease the risk of contact with infected body secretions, no one should assume that they provide complete protection. Moreover, even though manufacturers continue to improve this product, condoms can break.

Condoms are primarily designed to protect sexual partners during vaginal sex. They should also be used for all episodes of oral intercourse. Although they can provide protection during anal sex, condoms are much more likely to break during this activity because, unlike the vagina, the anus does not contain lubricating glands to facilitate intercourse. Anal intercourse is also considered risky because the delicate tissues lining the anus are easily torn, providing ready entry points for infection.

Condoms lubricated with sperm-killing (spermicidal) *nonoxynol-9* may offer additional protection against the AIDS virus. However, even though laboratory research has found that nonoxynol-9 kills HIV in the test tube, there is as yet no solid evidence that it does so during sexual intercourse, according to NIH. Nevertheless, the spermicide is known to protect against chlamydia and gonorrhea.

Condoms should never be used more than once, and they should not be used with oil-based lubricants such as petroleum jelly. These lubricants can weaken the latex and encourage tearing. Water-based lubricants will not harm the material.

In the early 1990s, trying to stem the rising tide of teenage HIV infections, New York City initiated a program of making condoms available to the more than 260,000 city public high school students, possibly the most extensive such plan in the nation.

STAYING HEALTHY

Everyone who is sexually active should have a medical checkup for STDs at least once a year. Anyone who believes that he or she might have been exposed to an STD or notices symptoms of such a disease should seek immediate medical attention. Private doctors and public health clinics can provide this care. In almost every state, doctors can treat anyone over 12 years of age for an STD without getting parental permission. Free care is available in every community for those unable to pay for treatment.

WHEN INFECTION OCCURS

Each year more than 3 million new cases of STDs occur in teenagers in the United States. STDs are illnesses, not crimes, and people who are infected should contact all of their sexual partners and make sure that they seek medical attention. Frequently, doctors will want to examine and treat all sexual partners of an infected patient even if the partners are not experiencing STD symptoms.

People who are sexually active should have a medical checkup for STDs at least once a year.

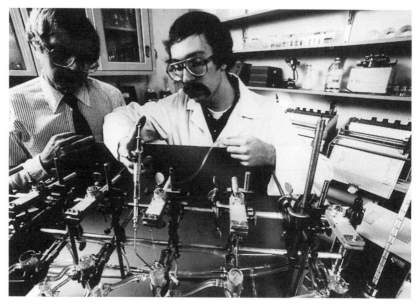

Despite the work of pharmaceutical companies to find new AIDS treatments, only a few drugs have been approved for therapy. They are not, however, a cure.

PREVENTION AND TREATMENT: THE FUTURE

In recent years, researchers have developed more accurate diagnostic tests and better treatments for STDs. Unfortunately, their work has done very little to slow the epidemic spread of these infections. As scientists continue their studies, it is reasonable to expect further advances in treatment; the development of vaccines for many STDs; a cure, or at least improved therapy, for herpes and HIV infection; and improved methods of disease detection in symptom-free people.

The most important work in gaining control of the epidemic, however, must be done on an individual basis. Until each person receives the information needed to understand STDs and takes necessary action to prevent exposure, millions more will suffer.

APPENDIX

FOR MORE INFORMATION

The following is a list of national organizations in Canada and the United States that can provide more information on sexually transmitted diseases.

General

American Foundation for the Prevention
of Venereal Disease, Inc.
799 Broadway, Suite 638
New York, NY 10003
(212) 759-2069

American Social Health Association
(ASHA)
P.O. Box 13827
Research Triangle Park, NC 27709
(919) 361-8400
Spanish callers: 800-344-7432
www.ashastd.org

CDC National STD Hotline
1-800-227-8922

Centers for Disease Control
Department of Health and Human Services
Public Health Information Service
1600 Clifton Road, NE
Atlanta, GA 30333
(404) 639-3311
(800) 342-7514
www.cdc.gov

National Institute of Allergy and
Infectious Diseases
National Institutes of Health
Bethesda, MD 20892
(202) 496-5717
www.nih.gov

AIDS

AIDS Action Council
1875 Connecticut Avenue, NW, #700
Washington, DC 20009
(202) 986-1300

HIV Network of Edmonton Society
#600 10242 105 St.
Edmonton, Alberta T5J3I.5
Canada
(780) 488-5742
www.hivedmonton.com

Bay Area Assoc. of Physicians for
Human Rights
2940 16th St.
San Francisco, CA 94103
(415) 558-9353

Body Positive
19 Fulton St.
New York, NY 10038
(212) 566-7333
www.thebody.com

Canadian AIDS Society
170 Laurier Avenue, West, Suite 1801
Ottawa K I P SZ5
(613) 230-3580
www.cdnaids.ca

Gay Men's Health Crisis (GMHC)
119 West 24th St
New York, NY 10011
Gay Men's Health Crisis Hot Line:
(212) 807-6655
www.gmhc.org

Haitian Coalition on AIDS
50 Court Street
Brooklyn, NY 11201
(718) 855-0972
(bilingual operators)

Hispanic AIDS Forum, Inc.
184 5th Ave
New York, NY 10013
Hot line: (212) 741-9797
(bilingual operators)

Minority Task Force on AIDS
505 8th Ave
New York, NY 10026
(212) 870-2691

National Gay and Lesbian Task Force
  Hot Line
1151 Mass. Ave
Cambridge, MA 01238
(617) 492-6393

U.S. Conference of Mayors
1620 I Street, NW, 4th Floor
Washington, DC 20006
(202) 293-7330
www.usmayors.org/uscm
(publishes *Directory of AIDS Related
  Services)*

U.S. Public Health Service
Office of Public Affairs
Hubert H. Humphrey Building
Room 725-H
200 Independence Avenue, SW
Washington, DC 20201
(202) 690-7694
National AIDS Hot line: (800) 342-AIDS
www.cdcnpin.org
www.ashastd.org
(Spanish-speaking operators available)

For information about where to go for
confidential AIDS testing, contact your
local or state health department.

APPENDIX

FURTHER READING

GENERAL INFORMATION

American Academy of Pediatrics. *Circumcision Policy Statement.* Pediatrics, vol. 103, no. 3, 1999.

Balfour, Henry H. *Herpes Diseases and Your Health.* Minneapolis: University of Minnesota Press, 1984.

Barlow, David. *Sexually Transmitted Disease: The Facts.* New York: Oxford University Press, 1979.

Boston Women's Health Collective Staff. *The New Our Bodies, Our Selves.* Rev. ed. New York: Simon & Schuster, 1984.

Brooks, George F. *Gonococcal Infection.* Baltimore: Arnold, 1985.

Centers for Disease Control and Prevention. *Sexually Transmitted Diseases Surveillance.* Atlanta: CDC, 1997.

DeCotiis, Sue, M.D. *A Woman's Guide to Sexual Health.* New York: Pocket Books, 1989.

Ewald, Paul M. and Paul W. Ewald. *Evolution of Infectious Disease.* New York: Oxford University Press, 1996.

Handbook of Diseases. Springhouse, PA: Springhouse Publishing Company, 1996.

Institute of Medicine. *The Hidden Epidemic: Confronting Sexually Transmitted Diseases.* Washington, DC: National Academy Press, 1997.

Llewellyn-Jones, Derek. *Herpes, AIDS and Other Sexually Transmitted Diseases.* London: Faber & Faber, 1985.

McCoy, Kathy, and Charles Wibbelsman, M.D. *The New Teenage Body Book.* Los Angeles: Price Stern Sloan, 1987.

Marieb, E. N. *Human Anatomy and Physiology,* 3rd ed. Redwood City, CA: Benjamin Cummings, 1995.

Merck Research Laboratories. *The Merck Manual of Diagnosis and Therapy,* 17th ed. Rahway, NJ: Merck & Co., 1999.

Morse, Stephen, et al. *Atlas of Sexually Transmitted Diseases.* Philadelphia: Lippincott, 1989.

Nahmias, Andre *J. Bacteria, Myoplasmae, Chlamydiae, and Fungi.* New York: Plenum, 1981.

Reeve, Peter. *Chlamydial Infections.* New York: Springer-Verlag, 1987.

Schell, Ronald F. *Pathology and Immunology of Treponemal Infection.* New York: Dekker, 1983.

Thomas, Clayton L. (ed.). *Taber's Cyclopedic Medical Dictionary,* 18th ed. Philadelphia: F. A. Davis, 1997.

AIDS

Fettner, Ann Giudici, and William A. Check. *The Truth About AIDS: The Evolution of an Epidemic.* Rev. ed. New York: Holt, Rinehart & Winston, 1987.

Hancock, Graham, and Enver Carin. *AIDS: The Deadly Epidemic.* North Pomfret, VT: David and Charles, 1987.

Harawi, Sami J. *Pathology and Pathophysiology of AIDS and HlV-related Diseases.* St. Louis, MO: Mosby, 1998.

Jacobs, George, and Joseph Kerrins, M.D. *What We Need to Know AboutAlDS Now! The AIDS File.* Woods Hole, MA: Cromlech Books, 1987.

Kübler-Ross, Elisabeth, M.D., with Mal Warshaw. *AIDS: The Ultimate Challenge.* New York: Macmillan, 1988.

Lerner, Ethan A. *Understanding AIDS.* Minneapolis: Lerner Publications, 1987.

Madaras, Lynda. *Lynda Madaras Talks to Teens About AIDS: An Essential Guide for Parents, Teachers, and Young People.* New York: Newmarket, 1988.

Martelli, Leonard J., with Fran D. Peltz and William Messina. *When Someone You Know Has AIDS. A Practical Guide.* New York: Crown, 1987.

Shilts, Randy. *And the Band Played On: Politics, People, and the AIDS Epidemic.* New York: St. Martin's Press, 1987.

UNAIDS: Report on global HIV/AIDS Epidemic, December, 1997.

HISTORY

Brandt, Allan *M. No Magic Bullet: A Social History of Venereal Disease in the United States Since 1880.* New York: Oxford University Press, 1987.

Brooks, Stewart M. *The VD Story: Medicine's Battle Against the Scourge of Venereal Disease.* Totowa, NJ: Littlefield, Adams, 1973.

Quétel, Claude. *The History of Syphilis.* Baltimore: Johns Hopkins University Press, 1990.

SAFE SEX AND STD PREVENTION

Breitman, Patti, et al. *How to Persuade Your Lover to Use a Condom . . . and Why You Should.* Rocklin, CA: Prima, 1987.

Mandel, Bea, and Byron Mandel. *Play Safe: How to Avoid Getting Sexually Transmitted Diseases.* Foster City, CA: Center for Health Information, 1986.

Zinner, Stephen H., M.D. *How to Protect Yourself from STDs.* New York: Summit Books, 1986.

APPENDIX

GLOSSARY

Acyclovir: A prescription drug used for the treatment of the symptoms of genital herpes.

AIDS: Acquired immune deficiency syndrome; an acquired defect in the immune system; the final stage of the disease caused by the human immunodeficiency virus (HIV); spread by the blood, by sexual contact, through nutritive fluids passed from a mother to her fetus, or through breast milk; leaves victims vulnerable to certain, often fatal, infections and cancers.

Antibiotics: The group of drugs, usually prepared from molds, which are used in treatment of specific infections by inhibiting or destroying microorganisms.

Antibody: A protein substance produced by cells of the immune system in response to the presence of a foreign or infectious agent.

AZT: Azidothymidine, or zidovudine; an antiviral drug; the first drug to be approved by the FDA for the treatment of AIDS.

Bartholin's glands: The two female lubricating glands located close to the opening of the vagina.

Bisexual: An individual who directs sexual desire toward members of both sexes.

Candida albicans: An infectious fungus that causes yeast infections.

Celibacy: Abstention from sexual activity.

Cervicitis: Inflammation of the cervix due to infection.

Cervix: The neck of the uterus; extends down into the vagina.

Chancre: A usually painless sore that develops at the site where syphilis bacteria enter the body.

Chancroid: A bacterial STD that produces a painful genital ulcer.

Chlamydia: A series of infections caused by different strains of the bacterium *Chalamydial trachomatis.*

Chlamydia trachomatis: The bacterium responsible for chlamydia infections and LGV.

Circumcision: The removal of the foreskin of the penis for religious or sanitary purposes.

Clitoris: The small and sensitive erectile female genital organ that protrudes beneath the mons pubis; homologous to the penis.

Condom: A cover worn over the erect penis during intercourse to prevent impregnation or infection; usually made out of lambskin or latex; only the latex variety offers effective protection from STDs.

Condyloma lata: Extremely infectious masses of lesions; characteristic of secondary syphilis.

Conjunctivitis: An infection of the membrane that lines the inner surface of the eye.

Cryotherapy: The therapeutic application of a substance, such as liquid nitrogen, that can freeze and destroy tissue; used to remove genital warts.

Culture test: The method of testing for a specific infection by incubating sample material and testing for bacteria; used to diagnose gonorrhea and other infections.

Dark field microscopic examination: A test for syphilis used to check for the presence of the bacterium *Treponema pallidum*.

Diaphragm: A thin rubber cap fitted over the cervix for contraceptive use.

Ectopic pregnancy: The attachment of a fertilized egg anywhere other than in the uterus, such as in a fallopian tube; accompanied by fever, bleeding, and extreme pain; may lead to infertility and even death.

ELISA test: Enzyme-linked immunosorbent assay test; can identify the presence of specific antibodies in the blood; an accurate test for the AIDS virus.

Epididymis: The narrow tubes that carry mature sperm from the testes to the urethra.

Epididymitis: Inflammation of the epididymis; often caused by an untreated STD.

Erythromycin: An antibiotic that resembles penicillin; effective treatment against chancroid.

Fallopian tubes: The pair of tubes, or ducts, that extend from the uterus to the ovaries and through which ova (eggs) travel from the ovaries to the uterus; the most common site for fertilization of a mature egg by a sperm.

Foreskin: The protective tissue covering the glans penis; often removed by circumcision.

Fourchette: A juncture of tissue formed at the base of the vulva, where the labia majora and labia minora come together.

FTA test: Fluorescent treponemal antibody test; blood test for syphilis usable during any stage of infection; measures presence of identifiable components of the syphilis bacteria.

Gardnerella vaginalis: A highly contagious bacterial infection of the vagina that causes discharge and irritation.

Genital warts: A highly contagious STD caused by human papillomaviruses; characterized by a warty growth usually near the anus and genital organs.

Glans penis: The bulbous tip of the penis; contains tightly packed nerve endings.

Gonorrhea: A common bacterial STD characterized by painful urination and a white or yellow discharge; more easily detected in men than in women; may be treated effectively with antibiotics if detected early; if left untreated, can cause long-term complications such as sterility.

Gram's stain test: The method of identifying bacteria using a solution that colors some bacteria and removes the color from others after all have been stained; used to test for gonorrhea and other infections.

Granuloma inguinale: A mildly infectious bacterial STD characterized by inflamed sores primarily on the genitals; most commonly found in tropical areas.

Herpes simplex: An STD caused by a viral infection; causes a painful sore or sores to appear usually on the mouth (Type 1) or anus and genitals (Type 2); can recur throughout a person's life; at the present time, no cure exists.

Heterosexual: An individual who directs sexual desire toward members of the opposite sex.

HIV: Human immunodeficiency virus; the virus that causes AIDS; its primary targets are cells of the immune system.

Homosexual: A person who directs sexual desire toward another of the same sex.

HPVs: Human papillomaviruses; a family of viruses that cause genital warts.

Hymen: A ring of tissue that partially covers the opening to the vagina.

Infertile: Not able to produce offspring.

In vitro fertilization: A procedure in which a fertilized egg is surgically attached to the lining of the uterus.

IUD: Intrauterine device; a device placed in the uterus to prevent conception.

Kaposi's sarcoma: A rare form of skin cancer characterized by bluish red nodules usually located on the lower extremities; frequently occurs in patients with weakened immune systems; rarely seen in the United States prior to the AIDS epidemic.

Labia majora: The two long folds of skin forming the outer protective lips of the external female genitalia.

Labia minora: The two folds of skin within the labia majora that form the smaller, inner lips of the female genitalia.

Laparoscopy: The visual examination of the abdominal area, particularly the ovaries and the fallopian tubes, by use of a flexible tubelike instrument introduced into the abdomen through a small incision.

Laser surgery: The therapy that utilizes a high-powered light beam to destroy infected tissue; a treatment used to remove genital warts.

Lesion: Any well-defined abnormal change in the structure of an organ.

LGV: Lymphogranuloma venereum; an STD caused by a strain of the bacteria that causes chlamydia; characterized by fever, chills, headache, weakness, and a swelling of the lymph nodes; an extremely rare STD in the United States but more frequently found in Southeast Asia.

Mercury therapy: A painful and highly poisonous treatment for STDs, now outdated; involved the prolonged administration of mercury, in a variety of ways, to a patient.

Molluscum contagiosum: A highly contagious viral skin infection that causes small, hard sores to appear under the skin.

Monogamy: A term that once referred to the custom of marrying only one person at a time; now often used to describe a relationship in which partners have sexual intercourse with only each other.

Mons pubis: The mound of fatty tissue in women that protects the pubic bone.

Neisseria gonococcus: The bacterium that causes gonorrhea.

Nonoxynol-9: A spermicide often used in contraception.

Nonspecific vaginitis: *Gardnerella vaginalis;* bacterial infections of the vagina caused by high levels of bacteria normally occurring in the vagina.

Ovaries: Almond-shaped organs located in the lower abdomen; produce eggs and the female sexual hormones.

Pap smear: A test for detecting cancer and precancerous conditions in the cervix; involves removing a sample of cells from the cervix; many doctors recommend that all women over 21 have such a test administered annually.

Penicillin: An antibiotic discovered in 1929; after first successful use against syphilis in 1941, became a widely utilized and effective treatment for STD, virtually eliminating such diseases in the United States for about 20 years after World War II.

Penis: The external sexual organ of the male; composed primarily of erectile tissue that swells upon stimulation; contains the urethra, through which urine and semen travel; homologous to the clitoris.

Perineum: The genital area separating the vagina and the anus.

PID: Pelvic inflammatory disease; a painful inflammation of the pelvic organs in women; often accompanied by scarring in the fallopian tubes and sterility; a common complication of an untreated STD.

Pneumocystis carinii: A type of pneumonia usually seen only in a patient whose immune system is damaged or not functioning properly; a common complication of AIDS.

Pneumonia: A viral or bacterial infection of the lungs leading to inflammation.

Prenatal syphilis: Syphilis passed on to an unborn child through an infected mother; can cause the infant's death or serious birth defects.

Proctoscope: A flexible tubelike instrument used for examining the rectum and the colon.

Prostate gland: The chestnut-size gland that releases fluids into the male urethra during the ejaculation of sperm.

RPR test: Rapid plasma reagin test; blood test for syphilis; can mistakenly react to the blood of certain groups such as drug addicts and pregnant women even when they are not infected.

Salvarsan: "The magic bullet"; the first effective treatment for syphilis; invented by Paul Ehrlich in 1909, remained standard therapy until the development of antibiotics.

Scrotum: The pouch of skin, lying beneath the penis, that contains the testes.

Semen: The mixture of sperm produced in the testes and liquid produced in the prostate gland.

Seminal vesicles: The small pouchlike organs connecting with the vas deferens; produce a solution rich in nutrients that nourishes sperm cells once they leave the testes.

Skene's glands: The female lubricating glands located close to the urethra.

Social Hygiene Movement: The Purity Crusade; early 20th-century social movement that attracted people to the cause of eliminating sexually transmitted diseases.

Sonogram: A diagnostic tool that uses high-frequency sound waves to produce an image of an internal structure.

Speculum: A medical instrument inserted into a body passage for better visual inspection; used by physicians for examining the vagina and the cervix.

Spirochete: A spiral-shaped bacterium such as the syphilis organism, *Treponema pallidum.*

STD: Sexually transmitted disease; a contagious disease transmitted primarily through sexual contact.

Sulfa drugs: A group of drugs that are used in the treatment of certain bacterial infections, such as LGV.

Syphilis: A bacterial STD that, if left untreated, can be fatal; once diagnosed, syphilis is easily treatable with penicillin; in recent years, the incidence of syphilis in the United States has increased dramatically.

Testes: The glands that produce sperm and secrete male sexual hormones.

Tetracycline: A group of antibiotic drugs.

Treponema pallidum: The bacterium that causes syphilis.

Trichomoniasis: A disease that can be spread both sexually and nonsexually; can infect the vagina and urethra.

Urethra: A tubular structure through which urine is removed from the bladder and transported out of the body.

Urethral infusions: An outdated, ineffective, and painful treatment for STDs; involved inserting narrow tubes into the patient's urethra and forcing various liquids into it in an attempt to irrigate the infected sexual organs of men and women.

Urinary tract infections: Infections of the urethra caused by microorganisms other than the bacteria responsible for gonorrhea; occurs more frequently in women than in men.

Uterus: The womb; the hollow, muscular female organ in which the fetus develops from the time the fertilized egg is implanted to the time of birth; connected at the upper end to the fallopian tubes and at the lower end to the cervix.

Vagina: A muscular organ lined with mucous membranes; the female organ that encloses the penis during vaginal intercourse.

Vaginitis: An inflammation of the vagina.

Vas deferens: The two ducts that transport mature sperm from the testes to the urethra.

VD: Venereal disease; alternate term for sexually transmitted diseases.

VDRL test: Venereal Disease Research Laboratory test; blood test for syphilis; can mistakenly react to the blood of certain groups such as drug addicts and pregnant women even when they are not infected.

Vestibule: Part of the external genitalia of females; an oval area within the labia minora that contains the urethra.

Viral culture: A method of distinguishing one virus from another; involves removing cells from an infected area, adding them to a healthy area, and watching for signs of infection in the healthy cells; the most accurate means of distinguishing herpes sores from lesions common to other STDs.

Vulva: The external genital structures of females.

Wassermann test: A test developed by August Wassermann and his colleagues in 1906; detects the presence of the syphilis bacteria in a patient's bloodstream.

Yeast infection: Candidiasis; most common form of vaginitis; infection of the vagina by a fungus.

APPENDIX

INDEX

APPENDIX

PICTURE CREDITS

Marjorie Little received her M.S. degree from the University of Pittsburgh and is a member of the American Medical Writers Association. Little has worked in medical communications for more than eight years, during which time she has written numerous articles for medical and scientific journals. In addition, she has developed a continuing medical education series on immunology for medical professionals and has authored a wide variety of patient infomnation material. Little is also the editor of *AIDS: You Can't Catch It Holding Hands*, one of the first books on AIDS to be targeted to teenagers. She currently resides in San Francisco.

C. Everett Koop, M.D., Sc.D., currently serves as chairman of the board of his own website, www.drkoop.com, and is the Elizabeth DeCamp McInerny professor at Dartmouth College, from which he graduated in 1937. Dr. Koop received his doctor of medicine degree from Cornell Medical College in 1941 and his doctor of science degree from the University of Pennsylvania in 1947. A pediatric surgeon of international reputation, he was previously surgeon in chief of Children's Hospital of Philadelphia and professor of pediatric surgery and pediatrics at the University of Pennsylvania. A former U.S. Surgeon General, Dr. Koop was also the director of the Office of International Health. He has served as surgery editor of the *Journal of Clinical Pediatrics* and editor in chief of the *Journal of Pediatric Surgery*. In his more than 60 years of experience in health care, government, and industry, Dr. Koop has received numerous awards and honors, including 35 honorary degrees.